The Making of an Atheis introduces the reader to a biblical analysis of the nature and roots of unbelief. While not disparaging the use of apologetics in laying out a case for theism, Spiegel shows that the central issues influencing disbelief are often more a matter of a commitment to moral and spiritual independence than to an objective assessment of the evidence.

> —**Greg Ganssle**, Yale University department of philosophy and the Rivendell Institute

Most of the work being done today in response to atheism focuses on intellectual issues and arguments against belief in God. In *The Making of an Atheist*, James Spiegel has crafted a clear, crisp, compelling case that there are non-rational moral and psychological dynamics that lead to unbelief. Rooted in Scripture and argued with the precision of a trained philosopher, this powerful little book is a must read for theists and atheists alike!

> —**Chad Meister**, Bethel College philosophy professor, author of *Building Belief* and co-editor of *God Is Great, God Is Good*

THE MAKING

of an

ATHEIST

●

JAMES S. SPIEGEL

HOW
IMMORALITY
LEADS
TO
UNBELIEF

MOODY PUBLISHERS
CHICAGO

© 2010 by
JAMES S. SPIEGEL

Published in association with the literary agency of Wolgemuth & Associates, Inc.

Editor: Christopher Reese
Interior Design: Ragont Design
Cover Design: Connie Gabbert, The DesignWorks Group

Library of Congress Cataloging-in-Publication Data

Spiegel, James S., 1963-
    The making of an atheist : how immorality leads to unbelief / James S. Spiegel.
        p. cm.
    Includes bibliographical references.
    ISBN 978-0-8024-7611-1
    1. Atheism. I. Title.

    BL2747.3.S695 2010
    239'.7—dc22

                                        2009045673

We hope you enjoy this book from Moody Publishers. Our goal is to provide high-quality, thought-provoking books and products that connect truth to your real needs and challenges. For more information on other books and products written and produced from a biblical perspective, go to www.moodypublishers.com or write to:

Moody Publishers
820 N. LaSalle Boulevard
Chicago, IL 60610

1 3 5 7 9 10 8 6 4 2

Printed in the United States of America

*This book is dedicated
to Alvin Plantinga—
a gigantic intellect
with a humble heart*

CONTENTS

INTRODUCTION

There is no one thing whatsoever more plain and manifest, and more demonstrable, than the being of God. It is manifest in ourselves, in our bodies and souls, and in everything about us wherever we turn our eye, whether to heaven, or to the earth, the air, or the seas. And yet how prone is the heart of man to call this into question! So inclined is the heart of man to blindness and delusion, that it is prone to even atheism itself.

Jonathan Edwards
Man's Natural Blindness in Religion

THE NEW ATHEISTS are on the warpath. They come armed with arguments to show that belief in God is absurd and dangerous. They promote purging the world of all religious practice. And they claim that people of faith are mentally ill. Richard Dawkins calls God a "delusion" and Christopher Hitchens declares that "religion poisons everything."[1] Some of the new atheists openly express their contempt for the Judeo-Christian God. For example, Sam Harris says, "The biblical God is a fiction, like Zeus and the thousands of other dead gods whom most sane human beings now ignore."[2] And Richard Dawkins describes the God of the Bible as "a petty, unjust, unforgiving control freak; a vindictive, bloodthirsty ethnic cleanser; a misogynistic, homophobic, racist, infanticidal, genocidal, filicidal, pestilential, megalomaniacal, sadomasochistic, capriciously malevolent bully."[3]

These are strong, disturbing claims. The new atheists do offer arguments to back up their proclamations—at least their less inflammatory claims. Unfortunately for them, they merely rehearse the same tired objections that have been offered up by skeptics many times before—arguments that have been repeatedly rebutted by philosophers and theologians, both Christian and non-Christian. There is really nothing *new* about the new atheism, except the degree of bombast in their claims. Their prose seethes with outrage. Their anger and resentment toward all things religious is palpable.

Yet the new atheists present themselves as having arrived at their conclusions through intellectual inquiry. And Christian apologists have been quick to respond to their arguments.[4] Indeed, it is tempting just to offer more of the same here. But this book has a different purpose. I want to show that atheism is not ultimately about arguments and evidence. The candid remarks of atheist philosopher Thomas Nagel are telling:

> I want atheism to be true and am made uneasy by the fact that some of the most intelligent and well-informed people I know are religious believers. It

isn't just that I don't believe in God, and, naturally, hope that I'm right about my belief. It's that I hope there is no God! I don't want there to be a God; I don't want the universe to be like that.[5]

These comments by Nagel, as well as those above by Harris and Dawkins, reveal strong emotions. Could it be that their opposition to religious faith has more to do with the will than with reason? What if, in the end, evidence has little to do with how atheists arrive at their anti-faith? Perhaps we should consider the possibility that skeptical objections are the atheists' façade, a scholarly veneer masking the *real* causes of their unbelief—causes that are moral and psychological in nature. That is precisely my aim in this book. Atheism is *not at all* a consequence of intellectual doubts. Such doubts are mere symptoms of the root cause—moral rebellion. For the atheist, the missing ingredient is not evidence but *obedience*.

The irrational heights to which the new atheists are willing to go in order to resist God are never more plain than in Richard Dawkins's speculation regarding life's origins:

If it were ever shown that life on this planet was designed . . . then I would say . . . it must have been some extraterrestrial intelligence, perhaps following Francis Crick's . . . suggestion of "directed panspermia" . . . that life might have been seeded on Earth in the nose cone of a rocket sent from a distant civilization that wanted to spread its form of life around the universe.[6]

Dawkins appeals to little green men as the creators of life on Earth, yet he calls *theists* delusional? What could inspire such silly thinking? How could an otherwise intelligent person propose this B-movie science fiction plot as a plausible theory? It certainly indicates that something other than a rational, dispassionate review of evidence is at work behind the thinking of Dawkins and the new atheists.

Atheism, of course, is nothing new. The biblical writers were just as aware of religious skeptics as believers are today. It is instructive to note the scriptural account of atheism. The psalmist says, "The heavens declare the glory of God; the skies proclaim the work of his hands" (Psalm 19:1), yet we are reminded that "the fool says in his heart, 'There is no God'" (Psalm 14:1a). Why? Because "they are corrupt, their deeds are vile" (Psalm 14:1b). In the New Testament we find precisely the same diagnostic. The apostle Paul does not mince words in making clear that lack of evidence is not the atheist's problem. Like the psalmist, Paul references the overwhelming proof of the reality of God:

"Since the creation of the world God's invisible qualities—his eternal power and divine nature—have been clearly seen, being understood from what has been made, so that men are without excuse" (Romans

1:20). So atheists have no defense or justification for their unbelief. The evidence is there; they simply refuse to accept it. Why? Paul's explanation actually appears earlier in this passage: "The wrath of God is being revealed from heaven against all the godlessness and wickedness of men *who suppress the truth by their wickedness*" (Romans 1:18; emphasis mine).

The biblical message is that there are moral dynamics involved in the abandonment of faith. The human mind does not neutrally observe the world, gathering facts purely and simply without any preferences or predilections. On the contrary, what one *believes* about the world is always deeply impacted by one's *values*. People are inclined to believe according to their desires; we tend to believe what we *want* to be true. Nagel's confession above—that "I don't want there to be a God"—is unusual only for its striking (and admirable) candidness. But the psychological dynamic it discloses is not unusual.

It is important to note that this is true for the theist as well. Most, if not all, believers want there to be a God. We *do* "want the universe to be like that." In fact, Sigmund Freud's famous dismissal of theistic belief as a wish projection turned on this very point. So does this even the score when it comes to the psychologizing of religious belief or the lack thereof? Hardly. Scripture breaks the tie, and quite decisively, as we have just noted. According to the Bible, God's existence is clearly evident in creation, while atheism is the product of moral corruption.

At this point, skeptical readers may be tempted to cry foul and accuse me of circular reasoning. Am I not, after all, assuming the truth of Scripture in trying to defend my Christian worldview, which includes the belief that Scripture is true? Yes and no. I most certainly am assuming the truth of Scripture. But my aim here is not to defend the Christian worldview nor even theism, for that matter. Rather, my purpose is to present a Christian account of atheism—an account that draws from the Bible, as any Christian doctrine properly does.

Christian philosopher Alvin Plantinga analyzes the situation as follows. God designed the human mind such that we would form beliefs through the operation of our cognitive faculties (e.g., judgment, memory, attention, reasoning, concept formation, etc.). When these faculties function properly in the environment they were designed for, we tend to form true beliefs—about everything from the physical objects in our immediate environment (e.g., I believe I see a tree) to moral and theological issues (e.g., I believe the world has a Creator). When it comes to the latter, human beings have a natural awareness of God, which explains why most people believe in some sort of deity. However, human beings are also "cognitively fallen" due to sin. Consequently, our minds do not always function properly. Immorality hampers our ability to reason correctly, especially regarding moral and spiritual matters. And the more a person indulges in sin, the more his or her mind is corrupted, sometimes even to the point that one's awareness of God is deadened. If Plantinga is right, atheism is a product of malfunctioning cognitive faculties.[7]

Some confirmation of the biblical approach to atheism comes, surprisingly, from an influential philosopher of science—Thomas Kuhn. Kuhn's landmark book *The Structure of Scientific Revolutions* introduced into popular parlance the now widely used term "paradigm." Kuhn's radical thesis—radical, anyway, relative to the world of the 1960s—was that scientists do not observe the world objectively but always *interpret* what they see in light of the scientific theory to which they are committed. Their theoretical framework, or paradigm, impacts all of their experimenting, data gathering, and analysis of results. Thus, even the most carefully constructed scientific research is biased. When data is collected that might threaten to undermine the paradigm, the scientist is likely to interpret the data in a way that is favorable to it. Scientists, Kuhn emphasized, are no different from other people, insofar as their values and beliefs skew their observations of the world. They, like the rest of us, tend to see what they *expect* or *want* to see.

Kuhn's claims, although controversial nearly half a century ago, are widely accepted among philosophers these days. His insights are helpful in explaining the resistance to evidence that people display in various contexts. This includes the atheist's resistance to the evidence for God that is observable in nature. From their own writings, I think it's fair to say that Dawkins, Harris, and Hitchens, no less than Thomas Nagel, do not want there to be a God. In fact, their antipathy to the idea is so strong that they find it repugnant. If Kuhn is correct about the way our biases steer our conclusions about the data, then it is no surprise that hard-core atheists should be so confident in their disbelief. Their atheistic paradigm has ensured that they see no trace of God, despite the fact that His fingerprints can be seen everywhere in the world.

In light of the biblical account of atheism—and its philosophical and psychological reinforcements—believers should not be intimidated by the new atheism. Nor should the church be deceived by the notion that atheism is primarily an intellectual movement. It is little more than moral rebellion cloaked in academic regalia. The new atheists are blinded by their own sin. In fact, if the term "delusion" applies to anyone who persists in a false belief despite its clearly contradicting the facts, then the new atheists are actually the delusional ones. (Let me hasten to add the caveat, however, that this does not mean we should ignore the new atheists' criticisms and insights.)

My thesis is an uncomfortable one. To suggest that religious skepticism is, at bottom, a moral problem will likely draw the ire of many people. But my goal is not to provoke or make people mad. Indeed, personally speaking, I would much rather write an irenic tome on the subject showing where folks on both sides of the issue can agree. (Actually, I do some of this in chapter 1, but that is not the overarching point of the book.) Furthermore, by turning the tables on the new atheists who claim that theists are delusional, I don't mean to be clever or cute. It is just an ironic fact that they have analyzed religious believers in terms that actually apply to them. In the end, my reason for making the claim I do in this book is because it is *true*. But, like all truth, I think it has many salutary effects, many practical implications that are helpful and encouraging to those who affirm it. For one thing, this means that theists need not be intimidated by the blustering claims of atheists and other religious skeptics. And there are many other benefits, several of which I will discuss in the final chapter.

The truth is that atheism is profoundly false. It is a misconstrual of reality at the most basic level. So it is no surprise that atheism has given rise to such harmful ideologies as Marxism and nihilism. But perhaps most tragic of all is how deeply irrational atheism is— a form of irrationality that itself almost defies comprehension. The reality of God is manifest all around us, from the unimaginable vastness of our universe, with its hundreds of billions of galaxies, to the breathtakingly complex micro-universe of individual cells, to the elaborate machinations in animal and plant physiologies and the diverse ecosystems they comprise. To this list we could also add the phenomena of human consciousness, moral truths, the existence of beauty, mystical religious encounters, miraculous occurrences, and fulfilled biblical prophecies.

To miss the divine import of any one of these aspects of God's creation is to flout reason itself. Yet this is precisely what atheists do, and it points to the fact that other factors give rise to the denial of God. Atheism is not the result of objective assessment of evidence, but of stubborn disobedience; it does not arise from the careful application of reason but from willful rebellion. Atheism is the suppression of truth by wickedness, the cognitive consequence of immorality. In short, it is *sin* that is the mother of unbelief.

1

ATHEISTIC ARGUMENTS, ERRORS, AND INSIGHTS

IN JANUARY 2009 some unique ads began to appear on buses and taxis all over Great Britain. The banners did not pitch a product, promote a new film, or make a public health announcement. No, these were commercials for a worldview:

There's Probably No God.
Now Stop Worrying and Enjoy Your Life.

With major contributions coming from the British Humanist Association and Richard Dawkins, organizers raised over £140,000 to place this slogan on hundreds of vehicles in England, Scotland, and Wales. The campaign was the brainchild of Ariane Sherine, whose initial aim was to counter the negativity of a religious ad she once saw that declared that unbelievers would spend eternity in hell. Sherine, a comedy writer by trade, said, "I thought it would be a really positive thing to counter that by putting forward a much happier and more upbeat advert."[1] Dawkins's statement in support of the cause was more acerbic: "This campaign . . . will make people think, and thinking is anathema to religion."[2]

A similar campaign was launched across the Atlantic by the American Humanist Association. Inspired by the original British project, these ads were rushed out in time to mingle with Christmas holiday festivities:

Why believe in a god?
Just be good for goodness' sake.

This clever twist on the "Santa Claus Is Coming to Town" lyric appeared on buses in the Washington, D.C., area. According to AHA spokesperson Fred Edwords, the goal was to make "agnostics, atheists and other types of non-theists . . . feel a little [less] alone during the holidays because of its association with traditional religion."[3] But, echoing Dawkins's comments, Edwords added, "We are trying to plant a seed of rational thought and critical thinking and questioning in people's minds."[4]

Whatever else these ad campaigns might accomplish, they clearly demonstrate the rise of atheism in public consciousness as well as a certain level of boldness among religious skeptics. Evidently, the new atheist movement will not remain contentedly bound to bookshelves and academic environs.

We'll return to these atheist advertising slogans later. But first we need to clarify just what atheism is and review the main arguments used by atheists to defend their position.

WHAT IS ATHEISM?

Some non-believers don't like the term "atheist." As Edwords's comments suggest, there are different ways *not* to believe in God, just as there are many orientations of belief *in* God. While the new atheists wear the moniker proudly, others prefer the slightly less coarse term "non-theist." Still others just aren't sure about it all and prefer the tag "agnostic" or, more generally, "religious skeptic."

Since this is a book about atheism, it's a good idea to clarify some of these terms before going any further. A *theist* is someone who believes in a personal God— an almighty, all-good, all-knowing Spirit who created and sustains the universe. Theists sometimes call God "infinite" because this denotes a lack of limits, and if God created everything (besides Himself), then He can't be limited by anything. Theists call God "transcendent" for similar reasons. Since space and time are aspects of the physical universe, the Creator must transcend both.

The term "supernatural" is sometimes used to refer to anything that transcends the physical world, including God, human souls, and angelic beings. And *naturalism* is the view that denies the existence of any such beings. All that is real can be fully described in terms of matter, says the naturalist. Not only is there no God, there are no angels, nor human souls, nor anything else transcending the physical. There is only matter/energy in space. That's it.

This brings us to *atheism*, which literally means a rejection of theism. That is, an atheist is someone who disbelieves in God. However, the term is usually intended in the broader sense of rejecting all forms of belief in the divine, including deism (belief in an impersonal god), polytheism (belief in many finite gods), and pantheism (belief that all is divine). Atheists almost always reject belief in the supernatural (including angels and human souls). This means that atheists are almost always naturalists. I say "almost" here for the sake of precision. But the truth is, I've never met an atheist who is not also a naturalist (and I know and have read plenty of atheists). Still, for all I know, there could be atheists who are not naturalists. But for our purposes here, I will use the terms synonymously.

Proponents of any of these views claim to know their perspective about God (or the gods) is the correct one. However, those who take a skeptical posture toward the issue are *agnostics*. The word derives from the Greek terms that together (*a + gnosis*) mean "no knowledge." So an agnostic is someone who simply does not know if there is a God. In its literal sense the term doesn't specify God as the object of belief (e.g., one could be agnostic about whether there is a highest prime number or whether the Red Wings will win the Stanley Cup). But this is the usual intention of the term. So an agnostic refrains from either affirming or denying the existence of God. For just this reason, the agnostic is partner to the atheist as a fellow *non-theist*.

To simplify my language in this book, I will use the term "atheist" to refer broadly to anyone who does not believe in God. This allows me to just use the term "atheist" rather than repeatedly referring to "atheists and other non-theists" throughout our discussion.[5] And, as noted earlier, I will also regard atheism as equivalent to naturalism. Given the above clarifications, hopefully even philosophically persnickety readers will not be too annoyed.

While I'm in caveat mode, let me make one more disclaimer. My purpose in this book is not to prove the existence of God or even to show that theism is more rational than atheism. I will note along the way some reasons why I believe atheism *is* irrational, but the ultimate point will be to encourage us *to look elsewhere besides appraisal of the evidence for the real explanation of atheism.* My concern is to explain why some people don't believe in God, whether they deny God's existence outright or simply confess to not knowing whether God exists. How does such unbelief arise? My answer, as I made clear in the introduction, is that the rejection of God is a matter of will, not of intellect.

THE USUAL SUSPECTS— EVIL AND THE POSITIVIST PIPE DREAM

How do leading atheists account for their unbelief? As one reads Dawkins, Dennett, Harris, and Hitchens, two principal lines of argument emerge: the problem of evil and the scientific irrelevancy of God. It is important to consider these concerns, and in doing so we will gain a better understanding of the atheist mind-set and the rational props with which they mask their rebellion. Again, I will subject these arguments to criticism not because I think the theism/atheism debate really boils down to a contention over evidence, but rather to show that something other than the quest for truth drives the atheist.[6]

The great novelist Fyodor Dostoevsky declared that "the earth is soaked from its crust to its center" with the tears of humanity.[7] Anyone who follows the news very closely is likely to agree. Indeed, even the happiest of human lives is marked by plenty of sorrow. Human suffering is generally regarded as "evil" because it is, as Augustine put it, a "privation of good" or, in other words, a departure from the way things ought to be. As such, evil includes both sin and suffering—immoral behaviors (e.g., lying, theft, rape, murder, etc.) as well as painful experiences (e.g., diseases, emotional disorders, natural disasters, and the like). Respectively, these are known as "moral evil" and "natural evil."

The classical problem of evil was first formally presented by the ancient philosopher Epicurus, and religious skeptics have offered it ever since as evidence against God's existence. Essentially, the complaint is that an all-powerful, all-good God would not allow evil to exist. But evil does exist, so there cannot be a being who is both all-powerful and all-good. Thus, the presence of evil seems to disprove theism.

The theist has two potential routes of escape here: either deny the reality of evil or explain why God might permit evil to exist. The first approach is really no option at all for anyone with moral sense. Who can deny that pedophilia and ethnic cleansing are really evil? Well, of course, some folks do, but this only shows they are as irrational as they are dangerous. For devotees of the major theisms—Judaism, Islam, and Christianity—scriptural affirmations of the reality of evil also rule out this approach.

This leaves the theist with the task of making sense of divine permission of evil, which is known as *theodicy*. Why does God allow the world to go so wrong—where people suffer under the terrors of hurricanes, cancers, and one another? Probably the most popular theodicy appeals to free will and the notion that we human beings have no one to blame but ourselves for our sin and suffering. God endowed us with moral autonomy that we might genuinely relate to Him, but we have tragically abused this freedom. So evil is our fault, not our Creator's. We act immorally of our own volition, and all of our suffering (from human malice to natural disasters) is the consequence of those choices—if not our own, then someone else's—ultimately tracing back to the first humans who brought about the fall.

Another major theodicy focuses on the greater goods that God achieves by permitting evil—significant virtues such as patience, forgiveness, compassion, and perseverance, which cannot exist without the substrate of some sin or suffering. One cannot be compassionate where there is no pain, and one cannot forgive where there is no transgression. Both natural and moral evils provide opportunities for growth in virtue and the building of a mature character. Still other theodicies appeal to such things as the laws of nature, divine punishment, aesthetic considerations, and the supposed need for evil to exist in order for good to be known.[8]

The objection from evil does pack some punch, and it is a genuine problem for theists. But it could never count as grounds for atheism. Even if successful, it only undermines certain beliefs about the *nature* of God. It does not—nor could any argument—

disprove the existence of a world creator and designer. This is because one cannot—whether by appeals to evil or anything else—eliminate the need to explain the existence of the universe. Nor does the problem of evil eradicate the abundant physical and biological evidence for design, as will be discussed in the next chapter. At most, evil should prompt us to reconsider what *kind* of God exists, not *whether* God exists. To give up belief in a world creator because of the existence of evil is a blatant *non sequitur*.

Secondly, and more fundamentally, from a naturalist standpoint the objection from evil is incoherent. This is because naturalists have no grounds to call anything evil. Why? Recall that evil is a privation of *good*, a departure from the way things *ought* to be. "Good" and "ought" are values, not physical facts. But naturalists *only* believe in physical facts. They have no foundation for a standard of goodness, without which the naturalist cannot judge any state of affairs, even the Nazi Holocaust, to be "wrong" or "evil."[9] And without a standard for goodness, the problem of evil cannot be posed.

Richard Dawkins sums up the naturalist perspective well when he says, "The universe we observe has precisely the properties we should expect if there is, at bottom, no design, no purpose, no *evil* and no *good*, nothing but blind, pitiless indifference. . . . DNA neither knows nor cares. DNA just is. And we dance to its music."[10] Here at least Dawkins is consistent with his own principles. He is, after all, a *positivist*. That is, for him, all knowledge must be scientifically verifiable. But, of course, science in itself knows nothing of values; you'll never find "good" or "evil" at the end of an equation or as the product of an experiment. While other naturalists attempt to sneak values in through appeals to intuition or the evolutionary concept of fitness, Dawkins rightly recognizes in this passage that this move is logically illicit.[11] He stands by his sworn devotion to science as the final arbiter of all truth. And here we arrive at the second pillar of support for atheism—the notion that science is sufficient to account for all of human knowledge and experience.

God and other concepts of the supernatural are not necessary for a complete worldview, says the naturalist. In defense of their view, naturalists often appeal to an important rational guideline called *Ockham's razor*. Also known as the principle of parsimony, Ockham's razor says that when attempting to account for some phenomenon, the simplest hypothesis, other things being equal, should be preferred. Well, says the naturalist, theism is more complicated than naturalism. Theists needlessly add God and other supernatural entities to their worldview, so it should be rejected in favor of naturalism, which is more simple and elegant (not to mention more intellectually fashionable).

Initial appearances notwithstanding, Ockham's razor does not favor naturalism. Other things, as it turns out, are *not* equal. Naturalism can explain neither the existence of the cosmos nor its vast instances of design (again, to be discussed in the next chapter). Nor, as we've already seen, can naturalism account for values of any kind. But it's not only naturalism as a worldview that fails here. The methodology driving naturalism, positivism, is also a bust. Positivists like Dawkins maintain that all knowledge must be scientifically verifiable. Admittedly, if that were the case, then we would all have to be naturalists. The trouble is that the positivist thesis is actually self-refuting. The notion that all beliefs must be scientifically verifiable is, well, not scientifically verifiable. So by the positivist's own standard, positivism must be rejected as unknowable. This simple logical point essentially defeated the positivist movement of the early twentieth century, though not before scads of scholars and their impressionable students fell under its spell. Dawkins and many others are living proof that, despite its embarrassing flaws, positivism is still wreaking worldview havoc.

As if self-refutation were not enough of a problem for positivism, the notion that science must confirm all truths faces another difficulty. Alas, all of us have many beliefs that fall outside the realm of science. And these are not trivial beliefs but some of the most important convictions we hold, from moral beliefs to judgments about love and the meaning of life. Holmes Rolston sums it up well: "Science is never the end of the story, because science cannot teach humans what they most need to know: the meaning of life and how to value it. . . . After science, we still need help deciding what to value; what is right and wrong, good and evil, how to behave as we cope. The end of life still lies in its meaning, the domain of religion and ethics."[12]

QUESTIONABLE SLOGANS

Let's return to those atheist ad campaigns. Crude as they are, the slogans actually raise interesting questions that have been the subject of considerable debate among philosophers. Aside from the obvious issues as to the existence and nature of God and whether or how God's existence is knowable, there are other questions lurking here that deserve our attention. First, is it really possible, as the first ad implies, to "enjoy your life" in the absence of God? Is genuine happiness feasible in a godless universe? Given the atheist's belief that there is no afterlife and, therefore, no enduring value or meaning to anything we do in this world, it is difficult to see how any person's life could be truly "happy." If only utter destruction and loss of all conscious existence awaits us, then this is grounds for despair, not happiness.

Although many atheists deny this gloomy implication of their worldview, some have dared to look this truth squarely in the eye. The distinguished British atheist Bertrand Russell provides a striking example:

That man is the product of causes which had no pre-
vision of the end they were achieving; that his origin,
his growth, his hopes, and fears, his loves and his
beliefs are but the outcome of accidental colloca-
tions of atoms; that no fire, no heroism, no intensity
of thought and feeling, can preserve the individual
life beyond the grave; that all the labors of the ages,
all the devotion, all the inspiration, all the noonday
brightness of human genius, are destined to extinc-
tion in the vast death of the solar system. . . . Only
within the scaffolding of these truths, only on the
firm foundation of unyielding despair, can the soul's
habitation henceforth be safely built.[13]

Richard Dawkins recognizes these implications of
his perspective. His response: "I don't feel depressed
about it. But if somebody does, that's their problem.
Maybe the logic is deeply pessimistic; the universe is
bleak, cold, and empty. But so what?"[14] So what?
Indeed, that is the question. Pessimism? Bleakness?
Despair? Those don't sound like descriptors of an
enjoyable life, which the British Humanist Association
and other contemporary atheists encourage us to
pursue.

The American atheist ad slogan, which enjoins us
to "be good for goodness' sake," raises another crucial
question. Can any sense of "goodness" be salvaged in
the absence of God? This question, in turn, can be further broken down in terms of two other questions, one

practical and the other theoretical: Can human beings find sufficient motivation to live morally without religious belief? And even more fundamentally, does the concept of goodness even make sense in the absence of God? Though we have already briefly discussed the latter question, it deserves more attention. But let us consider the former, practical issue first.

Since Augustine, many philosophers have strenuously denied the possibility of ethics without God. One of the more influential arguments for this view was proposed by Immanuel Kant, who maintained that there can be no genuine moral responsibility in God's absence.[15] Without a divine judge—not to mention moral legislator and executor—there can be no final accounting of our conduct in this life. And without a system of rewards and punishments whereby we experience the lasting effects of our behavior, there can be no adequate motivation to live a truly virtuous life, complete with all of the self-control this requires.

So what about the other question, whether we can even make sense of the concept of goodness without God? The answer to this question is well illustrated by another German philosopher, Friedrich Nietzsche. However, in this case the philosopher is not so much our teacher as an object lesson. In his book *Twilight of the Idols*, Nietzsche declares,

> No one gives man his qualities—neither God, nor society, nor his parents and ancestors, nor he himself.

> . . . No one is responsible for man's being there at all.
> . . . Man is not the effect of some special purpose, of a
> will, and end. . . . It is absurd to wish to devolve one's
> essence on some end or other. We have invented the
> concept of "end": in reality there is no end.[16]

By "end" here Nietzsche essentially means purpose, aim, or goal, perhaps best captured in the Greek
term *telos*. Now so far his assertions here are unre-
markable as atheistic diatribes go. But look where the
logic of his denial of God and human purpose leads
him just a few sentences later:

> My demand upon the philosopher is known, that he
> take his stand beyond good and evil and leave the
> illusion of moral judgment beneath himself. This
> demand follows from an insight which I was the first
> to formulate: that *there are altogether no moral facts.*
> . . . Morality is merely an interpretation of certain
> phenomena—more precisely, a misinterpretation. . . .
> Moral judgments are . . . never to be taken literally:
> so understood, they always contain mere absurdity.[17]

Here the granddaddy of all atheists, Nietzsche
himself, makes the point better than anyone else (even
better than Dawkins, whose Nietzschean stripes
should now be quite apparent). Without God there
is no inherent purpose or meaning to human life, and
without such meaning there can be no morality or

ethical standards. So "be good for goodness' sake"? Well, if we are to believe Nietzsche, this is a "mere absurdity."

The upshot here is that it is a mistake to think that happiness and goodness are possible given an atheistic worldview. Those atheists who propose otherwise, whether in academic journals or on bus banners, are confused. They would do well to heed the words of their more perceptive, if also more grandiloquent, forebears—Russell and Nietzsche.

The truth is that moral values and the belief that life is meaningful are borrowed capital for the atheist, borrowed from the very thing the atheist aims to demolish—belief in God. Meaning and value transcend the physical world and must therefore find their source in the supernatural. Good and evil are real, life is meaningful, and happiness is possible, but only because we have a loving Creator who is the definition of goodness and the source of eternal life. By eschewing all things supernatural, atheists abandon their only possible recourse for a meaningful and happy life.

WHERE THE ATHEISTS ARE CORRECT

We have seen that the standard atheist arguments are deeply flawed and that, furthermore, atheism undercuts the foundation for goodness and a meaningful life. What could explain the fact that intelligent people appeal to such poor arguments to justify their rejection of God, especially given the dire implications? As I will show in subsequent chapters, the answer lies in the realm of moral psychology. However, it is important to note that there are aspects of atheists' complaints that *are* reasonable and should be affirmed, even though they fall far short of justifying atheism. Specifically, atheistic objections are correct insofar as they critique many human failures that often occur in the context of religious belief and practice. The new atheists, especially Harris and Hitchens, emphasize these problems with force and eloquence.

First, under the general category of evil, there is the problem of hypocrisy. It is a truism that countless evils have been done in the name of religion. Theists of all kinds have acted in ways inconsistent with their confessed moral standard. In particular, as Sam Harris bluntly observes, "Christians have abused, oppressed, enslaved, insulted, tormented, tortured, and killed people in the name of God for centuries, on the basis of a theologically defensible reading of the Bible."[18] And many others who have not directly perpetrated these evils have been immorally complicit or refused to oppose them. Here we have no excuse and no recourse but repentance and a firm resolve not to repeat such extreme moral failures.

There is also the related problem of moral complacency. Christians—or those of us who so name ourselves—do not practice self-denial as our Lord taught us to. We are often greedy and stingy (only 6 percent of Christians tithe), slothful (how much television do we watch?), gluttonous (obesity is as much a problem in the church as outside it; and whatever happened to fasting as a basic spiritual discipline?), and lustful (the divorce rate among Christians is comparable to that of unbelievers, and pornography addiction is a problem in the church too). If I were an atheist, these facts certainly wouldn't endear me to religion. So I must ask myself, as should all people of faith: Does my daily conduct constitute a recommendation or denial of the beliefs I profess?

Turning to the general concern about the integrity of science, the atheists are correct in noting that religion has often been used as a pretext for shoddy scientific methodology. We need to avoid the God-of-the-gaps mentality, which is the impulse to appeal to God whenever there is a gap in our scientific understanding. This is sheer intellectual laziness. Inferences to astrophysical or biological design should be made only informedly and cautiously, when the possibility of any naturalistic explanation can be confidently ruled out. Naturalists' exasperation over scholarly failure in this regard is well justified and should prompt greater rigor on the part of theistic scientists.[19]

To these common complaints by the new atheists I will note two more that I have encountered among those who have left the faith. First, there is the matter of dogma and divisiveness about relatively peripheral doctrinal matters, such as the nature and purpose of baptism, the nature of hell, the question as to exactly who is saved, the practice of spiritual gifts, and views about end times. I have witnessed hurtful narrow-mindedness in the church about such issues, and frankly I can see why some are tempted to walk away from the faith community. At the same time many such faith communities are lazy about addressing practical moral matters, such as consumerism and racism, or the exercise of church discipline for church members who seriously flout biblical moral standards. And many churches fail to provide basic spiritual formation training for their congregants, teaching them to practice spiritual disciplines (e.g., fasting and frugality) that build self-control. Surely Christian obedience is at least as important as doctrinal accuracy. Our actions should clearly reflect this fact.

Another complaint I often hear comes in a variety of forms, but it can be summed up as distaste for some believers' refusal to admit mystery when it is clearly appropriate to do so. Let's admit it—the whole category of the supernatural is very mysterious and beyond our ability to fully grasp. Many of the attributes of God—His eternality, transcendence, and omnipresence—are brain-twisters; and the Christian doctrines of the Trinity and the divine incarnation are even more mind-boggling. We need to confess that we cannot fully explain or comprehend these truths. The failure to admit the mysterious aspects of these doctrines amounts to a certain disingenuousness, arrogance, or, ironically, even ignorance. There is no place for angrily dismissing atheists for their honest incredulity on these points. Many of these teachings are spiritually discerned and far from being so plainly evident as the existence of God or the Golden Rule. We theists, and Christians in particular, need to humbly admit mystery regarding transcendent theological truths, even as we confidently proclaim the reality of God and basic moral values.

The above complaints should prompt us to reconsider the way we theists engage in our moral, theological, and scientific practice. While they do not constitute reasonable objections to theistic belief *per se*, they are penetrating critiques of certain things people do in the name of God. In other words, these arguments accuse us of *theistic malpractice*. It is unfortunate, though, that the new atheists—and many of the old ones—fail to understand that the proper target of their best complaints is their fellow human beings. They rightly condemn those who abuse belief in God, but then they proceed to reject that belief rather than just its abusers.

It should be duly noted that the fact that there is such a thing as theistic malpractice is, in a sense, a confirmation of the Christian doctrine of sin. That there would be abusers of religion and Christianity in particular is just what we should expect if the Christian worldview is true. But this is no grounds for complacency. To the extent that the above complaints are accurate, we theists should be grateful for atheists' perceptiveness in pointing them out; we should be willing to repent of these errors, on behalf of the church if not ourselves individually; and we should guard against making the same mistakes in the future. In short, we should resolve to be truly good, for *God's* sake.

THE IRRATIONALITY
OF ATHEISM

IN DECEMBER 2004 news broke that rocked the world of professional philosophy:

> A British philosophy professor who has been a leading champion of atheism for more than a half-century has changed his mind. He now believes in God more or less based on scientific evidence, and says so on a video released Thursday. At age 81, after decades of insisting belief is a mistake, Antony Flew has concluded that some sort of intelligence or first cause must have created the universe.[1]

Most philosophers, including me, were incredulous at this announcement. Surely this must be a mistake, we thought. Antony Flew was not just "*a leading* champion of atheism" but the most significant atheist apologist of the last century. In several books and articles he had almost single-handedly altered the course of scholarly discussion of the rationality of theism. By arguing that atheism is the proper default position for the thinking person, he had put theistic philosophers on the defensive and set the counter-agenda for theistic philosophy in the West.[2] For more than five decades Antony Flew had devoted his professional career to the denial of God. How could he possibly disavow his unbelief?

In this chapter we will look at the principal categories of evidence that persuaded Flew to become a theist, and we will see why any fair-minded person should be similarly convinced of the reality of God.

A GOOD CASE OF THE FLEW
(OR WHAT A WONDERFUL WORLD)

In his fascinating 2007 book *There Is a God*, Flew explains his reasons for recanting atheism and affirming the reality of God. He writes, "My discovery of the Divine has proceeded on a purely natural level, without any reference to supernatural phenomena. It has been an exercise in what is traditionally called natural theology."[3] So, what rational evidences so moved Professor Flew? He highlights three main considerations: the laws of nature, the existence of the cosmos, and the presence of life.

Consider the first of these facts—that nature obeys

laws. Many folks do not realize that the laws of nature themselves need an explanation. But they do, because laws of nature are really nothing but regularities in the way matter behaves in space. So, for example, the inverse square law of gravity says that objects are attracted to other objects in a way that is proportional to their size and inversely proportional to the distance between them. And the second law of thermodynamics says that in any closed system, entropy (or randomness) tends to increase. These regularities are observable everywhere in nature. About this there is no doubt. But *why* are these laws constant? What explains the fact that we can count on nature to be uniform in these and hundreds of other ways? Most of us simply take this for granted. Scientists apply and formulize the laws of nature, but the metaphysical "why" question is beyond the reach of their field.

Among philosophers, whose job it is to address such questions, the theoretical options are surprisingly few—namely, necessity or God. Some take the "necessitarian" position, which says that the laws of nature are inherently necessary. The laws of gravity and thermodynamics, the ideal gas law, Avogadro's law, and so on could not be otherwise than they are. But this only raises the "why" question at a different level. If such laws are necessary, what *makes* them so? It was in light of this that Scottish skeptic David Hume refused any attempt to explain nature's regularities. We observe nature working in a consistent way, but we can't see "behind the scenes" to know why or how. No further causal explanations are possible. But to just give up and call it a mystery is unsatisfactory.

This leaves us with the theistic explanation. On this view, first proposed by Robert Boyle—the namesake of one well-known scientific law—nature's regularities can only be explained by the governance of a powerful and supremely intelligent mind. This is why renowned physicist Paul Davies has remarked that "even the most atheistic scientist accepts as an act of faith that . . . there is a rational basis to physical existence manifested as a lawlike order in nature. . . . So science can proceed only if the scientist adopts an essentially theological worldview."[4] And when one begins to understand the amazingly precise mathematical parameters of nature's basic laws, the reasonableness of this explanation only becomes more apparent. Antony Flew recognized this and eventually followed where the evidence unequivocally leads—to God.

Even more basic than the laws of the universe is the fact that there is a universe at all. The now well-established scientific fact that the universe had a beginning is a powerful pointer to divine creation. Astrophysicists tell us that about 15 billion years ago—give or take a few billion years—all of the matter of the universe was condensed into a single, infinitesimal point. Then . . . BANG (or perhaps BOOM, no one is quite sure which), the matter exploded at roughly the speed of light, and the universe has been expanding ever since. This Big Bang theory essentially affirms the biblical idea that there was a beginning to space and time.[5]

Again, those pesky "why" questions loom. Why did the matter explode as it did? And why was there matter to begin with? Regarding the latter question, Bertrand Russell and many other atheists prefer to answer the question by not answering it. The universe is a "brute fact," they insist, and we are wasting our time inquiring how it got here. Well, this is a peculiar attitude for someone such as Russell whose discipline is devoted to posing questions about *everything*. It is one thing for a scientist, *as a scientist*, to refuse to theorize on the cause of the universe, since this is really a question of metaphysics.[6] But a philosopher properly can and, in fact, *must* pursue this question. To refuse to do so is negligence. So while Russell and others might want to take their ball and go home before the metaphysical game begins, the rest of us must dutifully pursue this important "why" question.

The reason it is proper to inquire about the source of the universe is that we know it had a beginning. As such, the universe demands a causal explanation, since whatever begins to exist has a cause. One cannot reasonably ignore the question as if it were a trivial aside for the unusually curious. On the contrary, there is nothing more basic to human inquiry than to ask how all of this got here. Remember, the Big Bang theory only concerns what happened *to* matter, not where matter came *from*.

The cosmic question has become all the more uncomfortable for atheists in recent years with the growing evidence of the "fine-tuning" of the universe. To say the universe is fine-tuned is to say that there is an extremely narrow range of cosmic constants in which life is possible, and our universe exhibits just these constants. Imagine a radio dial that is billions of light-years long. (Good luck.) Now suppose that as you move the tuner there is only one frequency where one can pick up a station, represented by a millimeter on the radio dial. Well, it turns out, our universe happens to be "tuned in" to that station—the "life station," as it were.

Here are just a few of the many ways in which the universe is fine-tuned:

- The expansion rate of the Big Bang had to be accurate to within one part in 10^{55}. Any slower and the universe would have collapsed. Any faster and there would be no stars or planetary systems. In either case, life would not be possible.
- The force of gravity had to be accurate to within one part in 10^{40}. Otherwise, stars could not form, and life would be impossible.
- The mass density of the universe had to be accurate to within one part in 10^{60}. Otherwise, life-sustaining stars could not have formed.[7]

There are dozens of such physical constants that are perfectly achieved in our universe for the possibility of life. But note carefully: this pertains just to the *possibility* of life. Whether life could ever spontaneously emerge in our universe is its own daunting question, as we will see shortly.

Because of the odds against the formation of a life-friendly universe, it is not surprising that one atheistic objection appeals to the concept of *multiple* universes. Suppose ours is just one of a virtually infinite number of universes. If so, this significantly increases the odds of a universe forming with the right combination of life-permitting physical constants. The problem with this theory is that it is mere speculation. There is no independent scientific evidence to support it. It amounts to an *ad hoc* hypothesis aimed entirely at avoiding the implications of cosmic fine-tuning. As such, it is merely an article of faith.

The fine-tuning argument for God is strong and getting stronger, as the astonishingly precise balance of physical constants is continually clarified by science. For many folks, such as Antony Flew, the inference to God has become irresistible. But Flew's third major reason for abandoning atheism is perhaps the strongest of all—the impossibility of life emerging spontaneously from non-living matter. Even given a universe hospitable to living systems, one that is tuned to the "life-station," there remain insurmountable odds against life forming anywhere, even given the 15 billion years since

THE MAKING OF AN ATHEIST

the Big Bang. In the early 1980s two scientists, Fred Hoyle and Chandra Wickramasinghe,[8] calculated the odds of life emerging from non-living matter to be one in $10^{40,000}$. To put this enormous figure in perspective, consider that the number of atoms in the known universe is 10^{80}—a paltry sum by comparison. Moreover, consider the fact that statisticians, as a general rule, consider any "possibility" less than one in 10^{50} to be impossible.

Why are the odds so infinitesimally small? Hundreds of different enzymes are necessary for life as we know it, and for any one of these enzymes to be functional, a large number of amino acids must be sequenced in just the right order. As Hoyle and Wickramasinghe show, the odds multiply out exponentially, and this is just for the simplest of organisms. Thus, Hoyle famously compared the odds of higher forms emerging in this way to the chance that "a tornado sweeping through a junk-yard might assemble a Boeing 747 from the materials therein," to which Hoyle added that he "was at a loss to understand biologists' widespread compulsion to deny what seems to me to be obvious"—namely, that the infinitesimal chances of life emerging from inert matter show that it simply didn't happen.[9]

I want to emphasize that each of these categories of evidence for God—the laws of nature, the existence of the universe, and the emergence of life—is immune to the evolutionary objection. Natural selection *presupposes* the existence of living organisms, so Darwinism is of no help in responding to any of these evidences for theism. One of Richard Dawkins's oft-repeated complaints is that theists often mistakenly create a false dilemma between chance (or randomness) and intelligent design when critiquing Darwinism. As he notes, natural selection is *not* a matter of simple chance. Rather, an organism's fitness to its environment determines its survival potential and thus the perpetuation of particular traits. Here Dawkins is quite correct. But his complaint obscures the fact that the discussion need never get that far to settle the God question. Life cannot have started at all without a creator. In this sense, natural selection *needs* God. So the question of evolution is actually irrelevant to the debate about God's existence. Those who regard Darwinism as a shield against theism are deceiving themselves or others, or both.

Some atheists seek to sidestep the issue by referring to the emergence of life as "chemical evolution," which is nothing but a euphemism for spontaneous generation. Even Dawkins seems to recognize the flaws in this theory—the so-called "primordial soup" hypothesis—which was refuted decades ago.[10] This is why he seriously considers Francis Crick's "directed panspermia" theory, as noted in the introduction. As far-fetched (not to mention buck-passing—where did the aliens come from?) as this theory is, at least it is not as implausible as supposing that life sprang out of primordial soup.

There are further problems for atheism, even granting the impossible (that the universe, its laws, and eventually living organisms all emerged without a creator). Two of the more intractable ones are the emergence of consciousness[11] and the reproductive capacity of organisms (especially sexual reproduction). There are also the traditional criticisms of Darwinism, including the lack of intermediate fossil forms in the geological record, problems in accounting for the emergence of flight (in no less than four classes of organisms—insects, birds, reptiles, and mammals), and diverse instances of irreducible complexity in biological structures and functions.[12] But we need not dwell on these matters, since, again, when it comes to the question of God's existence, the discussion should not get this far. Once life appears, the only remaining rational debate should be among theists—as to how God did it, whether through special creation, natural selection, or some combination of these means. The issue of origins *should* be an in-house theistic debate.[13] But, alas, it is not regarded as such by the vociferous atheist minority. And this in itself begs for an explanation.

A BIBLICAL DIAGNOSIS

If the evidence falls so clearly on the side of theism, then how does one explain the phenomenon of atheism? This question can be very perplexing, especially since so many atheists are highly intelligent people.

This is why we must reject out of hand the notion that atheists are simply obtuse or feeble-minded. However much the new atheists—and some of the old ones—want to declare that theists like me are idiots for believing in God, we just can't respond in kind. Let's admit that both theism and atheism have their fair share of smart and not-so-smart devotees. As Christopher Hitchens observes, "There have been at least as many credulous idiots who professed faith in god as there have been dolts and simpletons who concluded otherwise."[14]

In light of the irrationality of atheism itself, the fact that many atheists are intellectually sharp suggests that something other than rational exploration is going on here. When smart people go in irrational directions, it is time to look elsewhere than reasoning ability for an explanation. And Scripture gives us clear direction as to where we should look. Consider the psalmist's declaration that "the fool says in his heart, 'There is no God'" (Psalm 14:1). The Hebrew term rendered "fool" here denotes a person who is "morally deficient." And elsewhere in the Old Testament Wisdom Literature we learn of various symptoms of this moral deficiency. The book of Proverbs says "a fool finds no pleasure in understanding" (Proverbs 18:2), that "fools despise wisdom and discipline" (Proverbs 1:7), that "a fool finds pleasure in evil conduct" (Proverbs 10:23) and is "hotheaded and reckless" (Proverbs 14:16). Note that none of these passages deny that fools can be intelligent or even very learned. What they do point to is a certain moral corruption that influences how they *use* their cognitive faculties. It is not intelligence they lack so much as self-control and the right values.

In the New Testament the apostle Paul specifically addresses the causal connection between the fool's moral condition and cognitive function:

> So I tell you this, and insist on it in the Lord, that you must no longer live as the Gentiles do, in the futility of their thinking. They are darkened in their understanding and separated from the life of God because of the ignorance that is in them due to the *hardening of their hearts*. Having lost all sensitivity, they have given themselves over to sensuality so as to indulge in every kind of impurity, with a continual lust for more. (Ephesians 4:17–19, emphasis mine)

The root of the problem, apparently, is not a lack of intelligence but rather a hardness of heart that is itself caused by immoral behavior.[15] Elsewhere Paul elucidates this pattern in greater detail:

> The wrath of God is being revealed from heaven against all the godlessness and wickedness of men who suppress the truth by their wickedness, since what may be known about God is plain to them, because God has made it plain to them. For since

the creation of the world God's invisible qualities—
his eternal power and divine nature—have been
clearly seen, being understood from what has been
made, so that men are without excuse. For although
they knew God, they neither glorified him as God
nor gave thanks to him, but their thinking became
futile and their foolish hearts were darkened.
Although they claimed to be wise, they became
fools and exchanged the glory of the immortal God
for images made to look like mortal man and birds
and animals and reptiles. (Romans 1:18–23)

In this passage Paul makes clear that the problem
with those who don't believe in God is not lack of evidence. On the contrary, God has made His existence
and attributes so "plain" and "clearly seen" from creation that unbelief is inexcusable. He also explains
how, in spite of this, some reject the truth, specifically
through immoral behavior. The evidential case for
God is not ambiguous, according to Paul. Rather, the
"wickedness" of the unbeliever works to "suppress"
what is manifest in nature. Consequently, the unbeliever's capacity for rational thought is compromised,
and this leads to even more wicked conduct. Paul
continues,

Therefore God gave them over in the sinful desires
of their hearts to sexual impurity for the degrading
of their bodies with one another. . . . Furthermore,

> since they did not think it worthwhile to retain the knowledge of God, he gave them over to a depraved mind, to do what ought not to be done. They have become filled with every kind of wickedness, evil, greed and depravity. (Romans 1:24, 28–29)

This is the downward spiral into sin, the vicious cycle of vice. Sin corrupts cognition, which leads to more sin, which brings about a further corruption of the mind, and so on. The overarching point is clear: immoral behavior undermines one's ability to think straight, at least about certain issues. From these passages, it appears the key subjects about which the depraved mind is blinded are God, ethics, and certain aspects of human nature.

A common way of thinking about the relationship between cognition and conduct is to regard beliefs as always determining behavior. We have a certain belief and choose to act on it. But the above passages suggest that it works the other way around, too. Our actions may also impact our beliefs as well as our desires. Some of Jesus' remarks confirm this idea, such as when He says, "Light has come into the world, but men loved darkness instead of light because their deeds were evil. Everyone who does evil hates the light, and will not come into the light for fear that his deeds will be exposed. But whoever lives by the truth comes into the light" (John 3:19–21).

The "light" here might represent Jesus Himself or,

more generally, the truth of God. And, as Paul would later echo, Jesus emphasizes the role of wickedness in preventing people from embracing that light. Note also Jesus' point that evildoers do not simply ignore or reject the light but actually "hate" it. If this is so, then we should expect some atheists to display a certain amount of bitterness and even rage toward the idea of God. And, of course, this is just what we find among many atheists, especially the leaders of the new atheism.

This is also what I have found from personal experience. Over the years—three decades since my conversion in 1980—I have witnessed the descent into atheism tragically played out in the lives of several friends of mine. Invariably, their "change of mind" about God was precipitated by some personal rebellion. The path has been roughly the same in each case: moral slippage of some kind—involving, for example, infidelity, resentment, or unforgiveness—followed by withdrawal from contact with fellow believers, followed by growing doubts about their faith (sometimes involving reading some of the new atheists), accompanied by continued indulgence in the respective sin, culminating in a conscious rejection of God. As this pattern would unfold, the anger and bitterness would also grow, both toward God and those who continued to believe in Him.[16]

I will not dwell on the sordid details of my friends' fall from faith. As evidence, it is merely anecdotal.

Suffice it to say that what I have personally observed confirms the model described by Paul in Romans 1. And my guess is that observant readers will recognize the same pattern in the lives of their own friends or family members who have followed a similar path.

We may summarize the biblical diagnosis of atheism as follows. The atheist's problem is rebellion against the plain truth of God, as clearly revealed in nature. This rebellion is prompted by immorality, which diminishes understanding, and a genuine ignorance results. This is not a loss of intelligence so much as a selective intellectual obtuseness or imperviousness to truths related to God, ethics, and human nature. But the root of this obtuseness is moral in nature.

It follows from the biblical diagnosis that atheists' arguments are an intellectual ruse masking their rebellion. The recent spate of new atheist books, like the entire history of atheistic publications, amounts to little more than a literary subterfuge. The flaws in their arguments are easily exposed—whether matters of bad logic or faulty presuppositions. These are further symptoms of their willful disbelief, which takes both this active form (presenting atheistic arguments) and the passive form of ignoring the myriad evidences for God, to which Paul briefly refers and which theistic apologists from Plato and Aquinas to C. S. Lewis and Peter Kreeft have tirelessly illuminated. Søren Kierkegaard puts it like this:

People try to persuade us that the objections against Christianity spring from doubt. That is a complete misunderstanding. The objections against Christianity spring from insubordination, the dislike of obedience, rebellion against all authority. As a result people have hitherto been beating the air in their struggle against objections, because they have fought intellectually with doubt instead of fighting morally with rebellion.[17]

While I would not counsel the abandonment of apologetic arguments as Kierkegaard would (indeed, such arguments were pivotal in the theistic conversions of such folks as C. S. Lewis and Antony Flew, among countless others), his point that rebellion is the root cause of atheism is well-taken.[18]

A SELF-DEFEATING WORLDVIEW

On the biblical view of atheism, rejection of God deadens the mind when it comes to theological and moral truths. Atheists are cognitively handicapped, and their quest for understanding is compromised. You might even say that, regarding certain issues, they are genuinely desensitized to truth such that they cannot perceive it even when they encounter it. Perhaps this is why atheists are unable (or unwilling) to perceive how their view actually undermines rationality itself.

Alvin Plantinga has developed an ingenious argument showing why belief in naturalism can never be reasonable.[19] Here is a rough gloss of his argument. He begins by noting that the naturalist must embrace Darwinism. This is because, in ruling out the supernatural, there are no alternatives to explain living organisms. For the naturalist, Darwinism is the only game in town. Now if the Darwinist story is correct, then everything about us formed through natural selection; every trait of every living thing is the result of survival of the fittest. Characteristics are preserved only if they provide a distinct competitive advantage in the struggle to reach reproductive maturity. And although genetic mutations give rise to various novel traits from time to time in evolutionary history, fitness is the *sole* determinant as to which, if any, of these genes are perpetuated in the gene pool.

Now here is where things get interesting. Given Darwinism, even our cognitive faculties must be the result of natural selection. Every aspect of human brain physiology and psychology was entirely fixed by its survival value. This means that nowhere along the human evolutionary path did a concern for truth necessarily come into play. So long as an organism's cognitive apparatus enables it to stay alive, its beliefs need not be true or even reasonable. There is no necessary connection between the survival potential of a cognitive system and the truth of the beliefs it produces. Does that sound implausible? Well, consider an example. Geocentrism—the belief that the Earth is at the center of the solar system—was a very *practical* belief for centuries, providing all sorts of benefits to sailors, farmers, and others who subscribed to the view. Yet, as we know, this view is false. Geocentrism was quite practical, though it was not true. Or consider this more fanciful example. Suppose I form the belief that the federal government will arrest anyone who has credit card debt and put them into prison. Consequently, I destroy my credit cards and pay off the remaining balances and live a much more financially responsible life. Not only do I not have to worry about being apprehended by federal agents, but I also am able to pay off other debts and even accelerate my mortgage payments. My false belief about the federal debtor's prison thus benefits me and my family. Yet, the belief is false.

What these examples show is that the *practicality* of a belief does not imply its *truth*. Nor does the practicality of an entire cognitive system[20] guarantee that it is aimed at forming true beliefs. This means that if naturalism is true, then we have no reason to be confident that any of our beliefs are actually true, and this *includes* our belief in the truth of naturalism. In other words, *if naturalism is true, then we have no reason to believe it is true*. If ever there was a self-defeating worldview, this is it.

Plantinga's argument here powerfully demonstrates the futility in the atheist's thinking, thus augmenting

Paul's point in Romans 1.[21] What could be more futile than a worldview that undermines itself? Atheism is a sort of suicide of the mind. A century ago the lovable curmudgeon G. K. Chesterton grasped this point intuitively when he declared, "Evolution is a good example of that modern intelligence which, if it destroys anything, destroys itself. Evolution is either an innocent scientific description of how certain earthly things came about; or, if it is anything more than this, it is an attack upon thought itself."[22] Of course, atheists do believe in truth and the general reliability of our cognitive faculties in forming true beliefs. But, as we've just seen, their naturalism cannot justify this confidence. This reveals yet more borrowed capital. Only theism, with its assurance that God has designed our minds to form true beliefs, provides adequate grounds for our assumption that thought reflects reality. Only theism can justify our belief in the truth of our beliefs.

Someone once said that "absence is the highest form of presence." I have heard this phrase applied to great artists, whose absence is sometimes painfully felt. But this assertion applies as well to the Cosmic Artist, whose "absence" is even more achingly apparent in the works and lives of those who ignore or deny Him. And this goes for the realm of logic as much as for ethics and spirituality. Even in His perceived absence, God is quite painfully present.

3

THE CAUSES
OF ATHEISM

THE ATHEISTS DISCUSSED thus far are all
scholars. But, of course, not all atheists are academics.
Like believers, they can be found in every sphere of
society. In fact, some of the more well-known atheists
are celebrities. Actress Jodie Foster, for example, has
spoken openly about her rejection of all things spiritual. In an interesting case of art imitating life, she
has noted the similarities between her own beliefs
and those of Eleanor Arroway, the astronomer she
plays in the film *Contact*:

> I absolutely believe what Ellie believes—that there is
> no direct evidence [for God], so how could you ask
> me to believe in God when there's absolutely no evi-
> dence that I can see? I do believe in the beauty and
> the awe-inspiring mystery of the science that's out

there that we haven't discovered yet, that there are scientific explanations for phenomena that we call mystical because we don't know any better.[1]

The late George Carlin was more emphatic about his atheism, even turning an anti-religion harangue into a comedy bit. Here is an excerpt from his 1999 HBO special:

When it comes to believing in God, I really tried. I really, really tried. I tried to believe that there is a God, who created each of us in His own image and likeness, loves us very much, and keeps a close eye on things. I really tried to believe that, but I gotta tell you, the longer you live, the more you look around, the more you realize . . . something is wrong here. War, disease, death, destruction, hunger, filth, poverty, torture, crime, corruption, and the Ice Capades. Something is definitely wrong. This is not good work. If this is the best God can do, I am not impressed. Results like these do not belong on the résumé of a Supreme Being. This is the kind of [stuff] you'd expect from an office temp with a bad attitude.[2]

So Carlin gave up his efforts to believe in God. He opted for atheism "rather than be just another . . . religious robot, mindlessly and aimlessly and blindly believing that all of this is in the hands of some spooky incompetent father figure who doesn't [care]."[3]

Notice that Carlin's and Foster's reasons for unbelief are founded on the two pillars of atheism discussed earlier. Foster's rationale for her view reveals a latent positivism, the notion that all knowledge must be verifiable by the senses. Carlin, on the other hand, provides a tart version of the objection from evil, which is as thought-provoking as it is irreverent.[4] But Jodie Foster and George Carlin have more in common than just being thoughtful celebrity atheists. They also share the experience of having lost their fathers while they were young. Before she was even born, Foster's father left her family. Her mother raised young Jodie, eventually guiding her into the acting career she enjoys to this day. Carlin also grew up fatherless. His mother left his alcoholic, abusive father when George was two months old, and she raised him and his older brother on her own.

Is there any relevance to the fact that these two atheists grew up without a father? Some recent research strongly suggests that there is. In this chapter we will look at evidence for the claim that broken father relationships are a contributing cause of atheism. We will also consider evidence that immoral behavior plays a significant role in motivating views on ethics and religion. We will see how desires often drive a person's beliefs when it comes to such issues, and I will propose that herein lies the explanation for atheism.

THE FAITH OF THE FATHERLESS

Paul C. Vitz teaches psychology at New York University. Though now a practicing Roman Catholic, Vitz was an atheist until his late thirties. Reflecting on his change of mind, Vitz observes that his "reasons" for becoming an atheist in the first place, during his college years, were not intellectual so much as social and psychological. Eventually, he began to focus his psychological research on atheism, and in 1999 he published the provocative *Faith of the Fatherless*, which proposes that "atheism of the strong or intense type is to a substantial degree generated by the peculiar psychological needs of its advocates."[5] Looking at the lives of numerous renowned atheists, Vitz's study reveals a stunning link between atheism and fatherlessness. This he expresses as the "defective father hypothesis"—the notion that a broken relationship with one's father predisposes some people to reject God.

While some might be critical of any attempt to psychologize the phenomenon of atheism, Vitz notes: "We must remember that *it is atheists themselves who began the psychological approach to the question of belief.*"[6] Turnabout, as they say, is fair play. Of course, a principal figure to whom Vitz's observation applies is Sigmund Freud, who maintained that religious belief arises out of psychological need. According to Freud, people project their concept of a loving father to the entire cosmos to fulfill their wish for ultimate comfort in a dangerous world. However, it was this same Freud who developed the concept of the "Oedipus complex," characterized by a repressed sexual desire for one's mother and murderous jealousy of one's father. Vitz notes that here Freud inadvertently provides

> a straightforward rationale for understanding the wish-fulfilling origin of the rejection of God. . . . Freud makes the simple and easily understandable claim that once a child or youth is disappointed in or loses respect for his earthly father, belief in a heavenly father becomes impossible. . . . In other words, an atheist's disappointment in and resentment of his own father unconsciously justifies his rejection of God.[7]

Thus, Freud's own theory can be used to explain atheism. And, as Vitz proceeds to show, the empirical data bears out this account.[8] The following are several cases from the modern period explored by Vitz that confirm his thesis.

Atheists Whose Fathers Died:
- **David Hume**—was two years old when his father died
- **Arthur Schopenhauer**—was sixteen when his father died
- **Friedrich Nietzsche**—was four years old when his father died

- **Bertrand Russell**—was four years old when his father died
- **Jean-Paul Sartre**—was fifteen months old when his father died
- **Albert Camus**—was one year old when his father died

Atheists with Abusive or Weak Fathers:

- **Thomas Hobbes**—was seven years old when his father deserted the family
- **Voltaire**—had a bitter relationship with his father, whose surname (Arouet) he disowned
- **Baron d'Holbach**—was estranged from his father and rejected his surname (Thiry)
- **Ludwig Feuerbach**—was scandalized by his father's public rejection of his family (to live with another woman)
- **Samuel Butler**—was physically and emotionally brutalized by his father
- **Sigmund Freud**—had contempt for his father as a "sexual pervert" and as a weak man
- **H. G. Wells**—despised his father who neglected the family
- **Madalyn Murray O'Hair**—intensely hated her father, probably due to child abuse
- **Albert Ellis**—was neglected by his father, who eventually abandoned the family

While this list is impressive, Vitz's overall case for his thesis is not limited to these but includes analyses of well-known theists from the same era. These scholars had consistently healthy relationships with their fathers or significant father figures. This confirms by contrast Vitz's thesis about their atheist peers. Such prominent modern theists include Blaise Pascal, George Berkeley, Joseph Butler, Thomas Reid, Edmund Burke, William Paley, William Wilberforce, Friedrich Schleiermacher, John Henry Newman, Alexis de Tocqueville, Søren Kierkegaard, G. K. Chesterton, Albert Schweitzer, Martin Buber, Karl Barth, Dietrich Bonhoeffer, and Abraham Heschel. Of course, none of the fathers of these men were perfect moral exemplars. Some, such as the elder Kierkegaard, grieved or disappointed their sons by their misbehavior. Still, the relationships persevered, and resentment did not prevail. In most cases, these men had strong love, admiration, and respect for their fathers or father figures.

To be clear, Vitz's thesis does not imply that having a defective father *guarantees* one will become an atheist. He takes care to emphasize this point. This is because, as Vitz puts it, "all of us still have a free choice to accept or reject God. . . . As a consequence of particular past or present circumstances some may find it much harder to believe in God. But presumably they can still choose to move toward God or to move away."[9] In fact, some people with defective fathers do not turn away from God but become vibrant believers and faithful practitioners of their faith. Given the strong majority of religious believers, it appears that most children of defective fathers manage to resist the temptation of atheism. Still others, such as C. S. Lewis and Antony Flew, give up their atheism even after many years of unbelief. So the psychological dynamics of atheism are very complex, but the impact of the father relationship does appear to be profound.

I would add that when it comes to atheism, *an explanation is not an excuse*. To identify a cause of a belief or behavior does not imply that the person is not morally responsible for it. So even if we can causally explain why some people reject God, this does not mean that they aren't responsible for doing so. Rather, the lesson seems to be that having a defective father presents special challenges to faith, but that this kind of psychological wound can only predispose one to atheism.

Now if Vitz's theory is correct, we could expect many atheists we know to have a defective father. This naturally raises the question, What about the new atheists? Do they confirm this thesis? We know that Daniel Dennett's father died in a plane crash in 1947, when Dennett was just five years old. As Vitz notes, losing one's father at such a young age is particularly devastating, since it is during this developmental period that a child bonds with his or her father.

Christopher Hitchens's father appears to have been very distant, so much so that Hitchens confesses, "I don't remember a thing about him. It was all her [his mother], for me."[10] Tragically, when Hitchens was twenty-four, his mother killed herself in a suicide pact with a lover. After his mother's death, Hitchens says, "I no longer really had a family," which is an especially sad statement considering his father was still alive. As for Richard Dawkins and Sam Harris, there is very little information available regarding their relationships with their fathers. Harris, in particular, has maintained such a low public profile that personal information about him of any kind is scant.

Whatever causal role having a defective father plays in one's becoming an atheist, Vitz has surely uncovered a significant aspect of the psychology of atheism. But *why* is the father relationship so important that its absence should create such an impediment to belief? We've already noted Freud's inadvertent explanation in terms of the Oedipus complex. But from a Judeo-Christian perspective, the proper explanation goes back to human nature. Human beings were made in God's image, and the father-child relationship mirrors that of humans as God's "offspring." We unconsciously (and often consciously, depending on one's worldview) conceive of God after the pattern of our earthly father. This is even encouraged in Scripture, as Jesus constantly refers to God as our "heavenly Father." When one has a healthy father relationship and a father who is a decent moral model, then this metaphor and the psychological patterns it inspires are welcome. However, when one's earthly father is defective, whether because of death, abandonment, or abuse, this necessarily impacts one's thinking about God. Whether we call it psychological projection, transfer, or displacement, the lack of a good father is a handicap when it comes to faith.

DELIVERY TO DEPRAVITY

The eminent twentieth-century historian Paul Johnson describes his *Intellectuals* as "an examination of the moral and judgmental credentials of leading intellectuals to give advice to humanity on how to conduct its affairs."[11] Thus begins a 342-page historical exposé that recounts behavior so sleazy and repugnant that one almost feels corrupted by reading it. Most disturbing are not necessarily the details of the sordid lives described by Johnson but the fact that the subjects are often regarded as intellectual heroes. Not merely successful people of letters in their day, they were scholars whose influence was, and continues to be, felt worldwide. They mastered their crafts as novelists, poets, playwrights, and philosophers and set forth ideals and values for ordering society.

So for most readers it comes as a bit of a shock to learn that so many leading intellectuals were self-serving egotists, whose ostensible interest in humankind generally was belied by their callous disregard for those nearest and dearest to them, especially family members. Among those examined by Johnson are

Jean Jacques Rousseau—intensely vain and wildly irresponsible; sired five illegitimate children and abandoned them to orphanages, which in his social context meant almost certain early death

Percy Bysshe Shelley—a chronic swindler with a ferocious temper; also an adulterer who, with three different women, fathered seven children whom he basically ignored, including one he abandoned to an orphanage, where the baby died at eighteen months

Karl Marx—fiercely anti-Semitic; egocentric, slothful, and lecherous; exploitive of friends and unfaithful to his wife; sired an illegitimate son, whom he refused to acknowledge

Henrik Ibsen—a vain, spiteful, and heartless man, caring only for money; an exploiter of women and contemptuous of the needy, even among his own family

Leo Tolstoy—megalomaniacal and misogynistic; a chronic gambler and adulterer; a seducer of women and contemptuous of his wife

Ernest Hemingway—ironically named, given that he was a pathological liar; also a misogynistic womanizer and self-destructive alcoholic

Bertrand Russell—misogynistic and a serial adulterer; a chronic seducer of women, especially very young women, even in his old age

Jean-Paul Sartre—notorious for his sexual escapades with female students, often procured by his colleague and lover Simone de Beauvoir

The upshot of Johnson's book is that not only do many leading modern intellectuals fail to live up to their billing as moral visionaries, but their moral perversity should cause us to question the legitimacy of their ideas. This is because one's personal conduct impacts one's scholarly projects. And, as Johnson shows, the works of these intellectuals *were often calculated to justify or minimize the shame of their own debauchery.*

Among the diverse vices that characterize the intellectuals studied by Johnson, brazen sexual promiscuity is the one recurring theme. So it is not surprising that most of these men explicitly rejected the Judeo-Christian worldview. Indeed, many of their scholarly and creative works openly challenged the values of this tradition, which condemns the sorts of lascivious behavior that dominated their lives.

Aldous Huxley, another significant modern intellectual, had much to say on this point. In the following quote he refers to a nihilistic worldview, but this could as easily be supplanted by Marxism, Sartrean existentialism, or Shelley's vision of a religion-free society:

> For myself as, no doubt, for most of my contemporaries, the philosophy of meaninglessness was essentially an instrument of liberation. The liberation we desired was simultaneously liberation from a certain political and economic system and liberation from a certain system of morality. We objected to the morality because it interfered with our sexual freedom.[12]

Elsewhere in this same essay, Huxley is even more candid:

> Most ignorance is vincible ignorance. We don't know because we don't want to know. It is our will that decides how and upon what subjects we shall use our intelligence. Those who detect no meaning in the world generally do so because, for one reason or another, it suits their books that the world should be meaningless.[13]

As Paul Johnson argues, the philosophical systems and social ideals of many modern intellectuals were decided by their will to be immoral, not their quest for truth. They wrote the books they did to suit their personal lives, not vice versa. This point is well expressed by E. Michael Jones, who writes, "There are ultimately only two alternatives in the intellectual life: either one conforms desire to the truth or one conforms truth to desire. These two positions represent opposite poles between which a continuum of almost infinite gradations exist."[14]

Jones's fascinating book, *Degenerate Moderns*, continues Paul Johnson's line of inquiry into the personal conduct of modern intellectuals. However, Jones does much more to show the connection between the academic theories of the scholars and their sexual perversity specifically. Thus, as indicated in his book's subtitle, modernism is essentially an attempt to rationalize sexual misbehavior. A case in point is anthropologist Margaret Mead, whose *Coming of Age in Samoa* was a bestseller when it appeared in 1928. In this study she aimed to undermine moral objectivism, the common sense notion that there are absolute moral values that transcend cultures. Mead rejected the Judeo-Christian sexual ethic, which she flouted by suggesting that even seemingly natural sexual standards are merely culturally conditioned. After studying the Samoans, she proclaimed that they "scoff at fidelity" and maintain a sexual ethos in which adultery is common but hardly a threat to their social order. Also, according to Mead, "the idea of forceful rape or of any sexual act to which the participants do not give themselves freely is completely foreign to the Samoan mind."[15] She concluded that Samoans "have no preference for reserving sex activity for important relationships."[16]

The impact of Mead's study was significant in Western culture, both in advancing the cultural relativist thesis as well as in reinforcing the social drift toward sexual permissiveness. However, it wasn't until five decades later that any scholar attempted to test Mead's study or corroborate her findings. When New Zealand anthropologist Derek Freeman finally did so, he found that Mead had badly misrepresented Samoan culture and sexual practice. The truth discovered by Freeman was that Samoans had fairly strict sexual standards and strove to abide by Judeo-Christian values in this area. They regarded adultery as a serious crime, even punishable by death. They highly valued female virginity; even those attempting to seduce virgins were subject to monetary fines. And rape was treated as an egregious crime.

How could Mead have erred so wildly in her depiction of Samoan sexual culture? According to Jones and other critics, the answer lies in Mead's personal values that she read into the data, whether intentionally or not, so as to reinforce her desire for the truth of cultural relativism, a perspective that affords complete sexual license. Lurking in the background were Mead's own sexual practices that were anything but Judeo-Christian. As her biographers have confirmed, she was a chronic adulteress and had a decades-long homosexual affair with fellow anthropologist and cultural relativist Ruth Benedict.[17] Her biographers, along with her personal correspondence with colleagues, reveal how these predilections impacted her research. Thus, writes Jones, "Mead's anthropological conclusions were drawn primarily from her own personal unresolved sexual conflicts."[18]

Another twentieth-century figure discussed by Jones is Alfred Kinsey, the famed "sexologist" whose *Kinsey Reports*[19] profoundly changed Americans' perceptions and attitudes about human sexuality. These publications and the public discourse they catalyzed helped to lay the social groundwork for the sexual revolution of the 1960s. Originally trained as an entomologist, Kinsey's interests turned to the study of human sexuality in the middle of his career in the 1930s. Desiring concrete data for analyzing his subject, he began to acquire "sex histories" through interviews, which he eventually supplemented with pornographic materials, including his own homemade films. Today the Kinsey Institute at Indiana University still houses tens of thousands of volumes of pornography and hundreds of pornographic films.

As an evolutionary biologist, Kinsey brought to his sex studies a heavy emphasis on variation, which had a predictable effect on his research methodology. It is one thing to explore a diversity of samples when studying wasps (an early research interest of

Kinsey's). It is quite another to emphasize variety when reputedly seeking to formulate an accurate picture of human sexual practices. Such "variation," of course, translated into deviancy in Kinsey's data acquisition. His preferred groups to interview when conducting his sex histories were prostitutes, prisoners, and homosexuals. And the data they provided maximized variation, thus skewing any account of "normalcy" reported in Kinsey's books. Or, as Jones expresses it, Kinsey's special research interests served to "predetermine the results he eventually got."[20]

Like Mead, Kinsey devoutly served the paradigm of moral relativism. In his words,

> Social forms, legal restrictions, and moral codes may be . . . the codification of human experience; but like all other averages, they are of little significance when applied to particular individuals. . . . Prescriptions are merely public confessions of prescriptionists. . . . What is right for one individual may be wrong for the next; and what is sin and abomination to one may be a worthwhile part of the next individual's life.[21]

Elsewhere he asserts, "Individual variations shape into a continuous curve on which there are no sharp divisions between normal and abnormal, between right and wrong."[22] Kinsey's conclusion here about the relativity of "right" and "wrong" is not only a blatant *non sequitur* but it transgresses the boundaries of his field as a social scientist. Reasoning about moral values is the domain of the ethicist, not the scientist. Such statements probably reveal Kinsey's deeper interests, which have less to do with the empirical fact of variation and more to do with, as Jones would say, rationalizing sexual misbehavior. Perhaps it was this radical relativist mindset that enabled Kinsey to justify his—even by today's standards—controversial data regarding orgasms in children from the ages of five months to fourteen years. Critics note that such research could not be conducted without either sexually abusing children or relying on the dubious testimony of child molesters. This is just one of the many controversies haunting the Kinsey sex research to this day.

As for Kinsey's own sexual conduct, this remained shrouded in secrecy for many years, but recent biographies have disclosed what reasonable people suspected all along—that Kinsey himself exemplified the sorts of sexual "variations" that he sought to discover in his "scientific" research. Biographers report that Kinsey was bisexual, that he sometimes engaged in masochistic practices, and that he encouraged his graduate students to engage in orgies and other sexual activities.[23]

While Kinsey and his colleagues were working to break down moral and social barriers to sexual deviancy, across the Atlantic another intellectual group had been championing a much broader vision for their sexual rebellion. The famed Bloomsbury group consisted of a wide range of writers and artists who have had a lasting impact on Western culture. Many members of the group, including novelists E. M. Forster and Virginia Woolf, painter Duncan Grant, economist John Maynard Keynes, and biographer and critic Lytton Strachey were either homosexual or bisexual, and the liaisons between them were multifarious. They saw their sexual practice as part and parcel of their broader moral-aesthetic vision that informed their scholarly and creative works. As Jones puts it, "For Bloomsbury . . . homosexuality and modernism were inextricably intertwined."[24] Keynes himself sometimes referred to modernism as "The Higher Sodomy."[25]

As with Mead and Kinsey, the Bloomsbury group recognized that their sexual practices could only be rationalized in terms of a relativistic ethic. Keynes represents the opinion of the group as follows:

> We entirely repudiated a personal liability on us to obey general rules. We claimed the right to judge every individual case on its merits, and the wisdom, experience and self-control to do so successfully. This was a very important part of our faith, violently and aggressively held, and for the outer world it was our most obvious and dangerous characteristic. We repudiated entirely customary morals, conventions and traditional wisdom. We were, that is to say, in the strict sense of the term, immoralists.[26]

Whether Keynes's choice of terminology in confessing that Bloomsbury was a collection of "immoralists" is completely sincere or intended as irony, it is nonetheless accurate. Theirs was a remarkable unity of thought and practice, the latter driving the former as much as the other way around.

In addition to Mead, Kinsey, and the Bloomsbury Group, E. Michael Jones explores an assortment of other twentieth-century intellectuals, including Pablo Picasso, Sigmund Freud, and Anna Quindlen. In each case, as with the figures discussed in Paul Johnson's *Intellectuals*, we see what might be called a historical-psychological confirmation of the apostle Paul's thesis in Romans 1: God delivers the sexually immoral over to a depraved mind. Jones sums it up well: "Sexual sins are corrupting. . . . The most insidious corruption brought about by sexual sin, however, is the corruption of the mind. One moves all too easily from sexual sins, which are probably the most common to mankind, to intellectual sins, which are the most pernicious."[27]

THE WILL TO DISBELIEVE

Let's review my account of atheism to this point. In the previous chapter, we noted the "biblical diagnosis" of atheism as resulting from a hardening of the heart (Ephesians 4:18) and the suppression of truth by wickedness (Romans 1:18). In this chapter we have considered Paul Vitz's thesis that a broken relationship with one's father is often involved in this process. But this is at most a necessary condition, not a sufficient condition, for atheism. It appears that the psychological fallout from a defective father must be combined with rebellion—a persistent immoral response of some sort, such as resentment, hatred, vanity, unforgiveness, or abject pride. And when that rebellion is deep or protracted enough, atheism results.

An especially devastating form of rebellion is chronic sexual misbehavior. Historical studies by Paul Johnson and E. Michael Jones corroborate Aldous Huxley's claim that the desire to justify one's immoral sexual practices has motivated many scholars to embrace cultural relativism and religious skepticism. Some noteworthy scholars have even gone so far as to fabricate data and otherwise transgress scholarly standards to win support for these views, which permit or even encourage yet more immoral indulgence. This is a formula, if ever there was one, for producing "a depraved mind" (Romans 1:28), as the apostle Paul puts it, which is capable of even "exchang[ing] the truth of God for a lie" (Romans 1:25).

But what of the role of the will when it comes to atheism? Recall Paul Vitz's emphasis on freedom when it comes to moving toward or away from God. Recall also Huxley's remark that "we don't know because we don't want to know. It is our will that decides how and upon what subjects we shall use our intelligence." Although Vitz and Huxley have little else to say on the subject, there are good reasons to emphasize this point. One great American scholar who would affirm this emphasis is William James, the nineteenth-century Harvard philosopher and champion of human free will.

William James was one of the most fair-minded intellectuals in modern history. He seemed wired to resist extremes and deal even-handedly with every perspective. This quality served him well at a time and place in American history that was rife with extremes, from the emotional tumult of religious fanaticism to the cool-headed skepticism of scientific empiricism. Meanwhile, somewhere in the middle was James, applying a pragmatic method of analysis to every question under the philosophical sun.

No doubt it was in part because of James's gift for fair-mindedness that he was invited to present the 1901–02 Gifford Lectures on that most controversial of all subjects—religious experience. These lectures, published as *The Varieties of Religious Experience*, became a classic text and over a century later remain the definitive psychological treatment of the subject. Perhaps what is most remarkable about James's study is that, despite his empirical bent, he not only remained open to the veracity of the hundreds of reports of spiritual encounters chronicled in his research, but he actually concludes by noting his belief in the supernatural:

The further limits of our being plunge, it seems to me, into an altogether other dimension of existence from the sensible and merely "understandable" world. Name it the mystical region, or the supernatural region, whichever you choose. So far as our ideal impulses originate in this region . . . we belong to it in a more intimate sense than that in which we belong to the visible world.[28]

James's openness to the supernatural irked his fellow pragmatists, most notably his hard-core naturalist colleague John Dewey, who remained a firm atheist until the end. But it wasn't only positive evidence for the supernatural that persuaded William James. There was a more basic psychological insight that drove him. James argued that there are significant truths in life, many of them practical in nature, which cannot be seen or understood *until* one believes. Likewise, one may willfully refuse to believe certain truths, even when there is strong evidence for them.

James makes his point using the illustration of a mountain climber who is unsure as to whether he can make it safely across a difficult pass. If he succeeds, he will go on to safety. But if he fails, death awaits. Can he make it? He will never *know* either way until he actually ventures. James makes a similar point about many philosophical issues, where the evidence alone is inconclusive. The lesson he draws is that faith is practically necessary. He concludes: "In the average man . . . the power to trust, to risk a little beyond the evidence, is an essential function. . . . We cannot live or think at all without some degree of faith."[29]

James's insight on the practical necessity of faith points to the crucial role played by the will and personal desires when it comes to belief. One of the absurd dogmas of the modern period—which, alas, remains alive and well in the academy today—was that the will is or, at any rate, can be perfectly neutral when it comes to the formation of belief. As a master psychologist, James saw the foolishness of this notion. In his short but influential essay, "The Will to Believe," James explains how this is especially the case when it comes to belief in the reality of moral values. He declares, "If your heart does not want a world of moral reality, your head will assuredly never make you believe in one."[30]

More than a century after these words were penned, James's insight is not very controversial, especially in our postmodern intellectual milieu, which prizes the diminution of reason in the formation of beliefs. But, of course, the new atheists are anything but postmodern. In fact, they are fierce modernists who regard the scientific method as the final tribunal of all truth claims. To them, James's thesis about the will to believe (or to disbelieve) is no doubt bothersome. How much more so, then, must be the words of fellow atheists who confess this psychological dynamic in themselves when it comes to God. Recall the candid reflections of philosopher Thomas Nagel: "I want atheism to be true. . . . It isn't just that I don't believe in God, and, naturally, hope that I'm right about my belief. It's that I hope there is no God! I don't want there to be a God; I don't want the universe to be like that."[31] Nagel is to be commended for his honesty, though it is a shame that as a philosopher he should so blatantly subjugate his quest for truth to his personal desires. One can only wonder why he doesn't want the universe "to be like that."

There is also the popular author and educator Mortimer Adler, who recognized that the nature of religious belief is such that it "lies in the state of one's will, not in the state of one's mind." Adler rejected religious commitment because it "would require a radical change in my way of life, a basic alteration in the direction of day-to-day choices as well as in the ultimate objectives to be sought or hoped for. . . . The simple truth of the matter is that I did not wish to live up to being a genuinely religious person."[32] Happily, Adler did not reject the faith his entire life but converted to Christianity in his eighties.

Recently *Slate* editor David Plotz provided another confirmation of James's thesis. Reflecting on his reading of the Old Testament, Plotz says, "How do I as a Jew cling to a God who seems to be so unmerciful so much of the time and so cruel so much of the time? That's very troubling. Do I want such a God to exist? I don't know that I do."[33] In one sense, Plotz's point is quite understandable. Who wants to believe in an unmerciful and cruel deity? But notice his apparent willingness to reject belief *even if such a deity does exist*. This is a conscious choice on his part and another case in point when it comes to the will to deny God.

To the frank testimonies of these intellectuals we can add many of the cases chronicled by Johnson and Jones that well illustrate the "will to believe"—or, in this case, the will to disbelieve—when it comes to God and religious faith. Atheists ultimately *choose* not to believe in God. But, as we have seen, this choice does not occur in a psychological vacuum. It is made in response to deep challenges to faith, such as defective fathers and perhaps other emotional or psychological trials. Nor is the choice made in a moral vacuum. Sin and its consequences also impact the will in significant ways (as will be discussed further in the next chapter). These moral-psychological dynamics make it possible to deny the reality of the divine without any (or much) sense of incoherence in one's worldview. This constitutes the general pattern of the rejection of God and all things religious.

Therefore, however much an atheist scholar, celebrity, or layperson might insist that his or her foundational "reason" for rejecting God is the problem of evil or the scientific irrelevance of the supernatural or some other "rational" consideration, this is only a ruse, a conceptual smoke screen to mask the real issue—personal rebellion. Admirably, some thinkers, such as Nagel and Adler, have admitted that their spurning of faith is based in the will, not reason. Most atheists refuse to admit this. However, as we will see shortly, there are factors involved in the psychology of atheism that make it surprising that anyone would recognize their own will to disbelieve.

THE OBSTINACY
OF ATHEISM

IN THE FILM *The Sixth Sense*, child psychologist Malcolm Crowe tries to help a small boy, Cole Sear, who is tormented by ghosts. "I see dead people," he tells Dr. Crowe, and "some of them don't know they're dead." Malcolm doesn't believe him at first, but he eventually discovers that Cole is telling the truth and takes creative steps to help the boy. However, the story turns out to be as much about Malcolm as Cole. [*Spoiler alert!*] For, as we discover in the end, Malcolm Crowe is himself a ghost. Having been shot to death two years earlier by a former client, Malcolm is now one of those dead people who does not know he is dead.[1] With this stunning realization, he is forced to reinterpret his experiences of the last few months with Cole and everyone else he has encountered.

This story can be used as an analogy for spiritual

awakening. After conversion or enlightenment, one's view and experience of the world is dramatically different than it was prior to the change. Conversion demands a reinterpretation of one's entire life, complete with a change of foundational beliefs, values, and ultimate commitments. For Christian conversion, in particular, *The Sixth Sense* story line offers even further analogies. "To be dead and not know it" describes the condition into which every human being is born— original sin. According to orthodox Christian theology, everyone is born spiritually dead and must be made alive in Christ. A stultifying aspect of this condition is that it prevents us from recognizing the condition we are in. Our spiritual deadness ensures that we can't discover our spiritual deadness. Not on our own, anyway. We all need a Cole Sear to somehow alert us to our condition, however subtle or fumbling those efforts might be. Then, and only then, can we glimpse the truth about ourselves and—to break from the analogy of the film—experience spiritual resurrection.[2]

In the previous chapters we have noted how atheists willfully reject God despite the fact that the entire universe proclaims His existence. And we have noted how immoral practices reinforce this will to disbelieve. For such a person, one's experience of the world must be vastly different from that of believers, who maintain a keen awareness of God. In light of this, it is no wonder that theists and atheists call one another "delusional." When someone believes in an entity that doesn't exist and even orders his or her life around this fiction, well, that is delusional. Similarly, if someone fails to recognize the existence of an entity that is ever-present and perfectly apparent to healthy-minded people, that too is delusional.

In this chapter I will discuss some ways in which a person may become locked in the atheistic delusion, specifically through the influence of worldview and the corrupting impact of sin on the mind. Both factors deaden the person's natural awareness of God, thus reinforcing the will to disbelieve and entrenching the atheist in his perspective.

PARADIGMS AND DIFFERENT WORLDS

The nineteenth-century German scholar Friedrich Max Müller once had a debate with a houseguest about teleology in nature. Exasperated at his friend's views, Müller declared, "If you say that all is not made by design . . . then you may be in the same house but you are not in the same world with me."[3] This well describes the feelings of people on both sides of the theism/atheism divide. People on both sides wish that the others would have a Malcolm Crowe moment and wake up to the reality of their true condition.

Although Müller was using a figure of speech, there is a sense in which people with such contrasting worldviews do dwell in different worlds. Their radically different perspectives make it seem so anyway. Perfect objectivity is impossible, at least for mere mortals. Yet some persist in claiming that science gives us an objective, unfiltered view of the world. Apparently these benighted folks have never read Thomas Kuhn, whose now classic book *The Structure of Scientific Revolutions* should have put to rest once and for all the naïve notion that scientists are somehow immune to the influence of their own beliefs and values as they do their research and theory formulation. But then again, most of us are fed an idealistic image of science and scientists from the earliest years of grade school, which is very difficult to shake. We are conditioned to think of scientists (the best of them, anyway) as unbiased, dispassionate, purely logical, Spock-like[4] automatons who simply report the facts and devise general theories, without any ulterior motives or besetting influences to interfere with their work. None of us explicitly affirm such a starry-eyed view, but the impression that scientists are somehow more objective, more dispassionate, and more rational than the general population or even other scholars is still very strong in the West.

Enter Thomas Samuel Kuhn, a physicist who also became a superb historian. His research into the history of science revealed that not only is this popular view of science specious, but the notion that scientists are routinely objective in their research is quite mistaken. Using dozens of historical cases, Kuhn showed that researchers are often far from neutral when it comes to testing and evaluating results. Rather, they tend to hold tenaciously to their theories, even in spite of contradictory data.

Kuhn introduced the concept of a "paradigm"— a set of assumptions, definitions, laws, and techniques that are shared by the members of a scientific community. One might think of a scientific paradigm as a theoretical framework plus the problem-solving methods of a particular scientific tradition. Some of the current reigning scientific paradigms include general and special relativity, quantum atomic theory, and Darwinism. The paradigms they replaced are, respectively, Newtonian physics, Bohr's atomic theory, and special creationism. Each of these scientific traditions offers a way of interpreting and organizing research data *and* ways of solving problems that arise within the paradigm.

Scientific paradigms don't come into being on their own. They are creatures of the human mind. Scientists "dream them up," as it were, to account for the phenomena of nature. (This is why it has been said that a scientist's most important tool is a good imagination.) As such, paradigms are always imperfect, subject to revision and replacement. And this, says Kuhn, is how the history of science proceeds—through a series of theoretical revolutions or "paradigm shifts." This is because each paradigm has its own unique standards for what counts as scientific truth. To use Kuhn's term, paradigms are *incommensurable*, meaning they cannot be compared by a single standard (or, as one might say, any two paradigms are "like apples and oranges"). So, according to Kuhn, paradigm shifts constitute a "gestalt switch"—the change must be made as a whole, or not at all. He uses the now famous illustration of the duck/rabbit (see below). Notice that while you can see the figure as a duck or a rabbit, you *cannot* see it simultaneously as both. A wholesale conversion of perspective is necessary to shift from one to the other. This is the gestalt switch.

During any period of history, certain paradigms are dominant in various fields. Take geocentrism, for example. For centuries it was believed that the Earth was at the center of the universe, orbited by the sun and other planets. But with the invention and continual improvement of the telescope in the early modern period, new data emerged that created a crisis for geocentrism. Servants of this dominant paradigm labored to save it and were forced to be creative when telescopic observations revealed that certain planets appeared to stop and start again in their supposed orbits around the earth. The geocentrists' innovation: the epicycle—a more dignified term for a "loop de loop." Then, as planetary motions became even more erratic, there came the epi-epicycle ("loop de loop de loop"?) and so on. Meanwhile, the heliocentrists (Galileo and others who believed Earth and the other planets orbit the sun) flaunted the elegance of their paradigm, which posited smooth, elliptical planetary orbits. And this pretty much signaled the end of geocentrism. But not immediately.

Old paradigms die hard, especially when they are backed by a Magisterium that reads Aristotelian physics (complete with geocentrist implications) *into* the Bible and then proclaims on the pretense of scriptural authority that God says Earth is at the center of the universe. Still, we heliocentrists might think, "Why were they so stubborn? Why couldn't those geocentrists, including both church leaders and scientists, see the truth?" But let's suppose you are put into a time machine and transported to the year 1510. After recovering from the trip, which would no doubt be exhausting, you get to know the locals and notice that they use the terms "sunrise" and "sunset" literally. This bothers you and, being a champion of truth, you decide to challenge them on this point. Since the matter has already been debated for millennia even by the early sixteenth century, they are prepared with a response. "Look up at the sky, simpleton. What do you see? Is that not the sun slowly moving above us?" To which you respond, "Well, yes, the sun is moving across the sky, but that is indirect evidence of the Earth spinning on its axis." This draws some snickers and a few hearty guffaws, and someone even remarks derisively, "What *world* are you living in?"

Fast-forward four hundred years from there (and, again, take time to recover because travelling forward in time is even more tiring). You find yourself in Austria in 1910 and you are listening to a conversation among leading scientists about a reputedly foolish young man who has proposed something preposterous—the notion that time and space are not absolute but *relative* to velocity and gravity. One of them exclaims, "What nerve to challenge the iron-clad truth of Newton's principles!" "That numskull"—or *Der Hohlkopf* in German—"will never amount to anything," another smugly declares. The numskull's name: Albert Einstein. More snickers, guffaws, and, again, the rhetorical question: "What *world* is he living in?" But after your experience with the geocentrists just minutes (or centuries) earlier, you know better than to try to dissuade them.

Disturbed by these experiences, you climb back into your time machine, speed forward another century, and return to the rational warmth of the twenty-first century. Unfortunately, in your haste you make a mistake in setting the spatial coordinates, so instead of landing in your backyard, you are plopped down in the middle of the St. Louis Zoo. Close enough, you figure. To let off some steam, you decide to spend a few hours there before heading home. And as you peruse the fantastic variety of animals, you overhear conflicting comments. Some say things like, "Look at the amazing creatures that natural selection can produce!" and "Evolution may be blind, but it sure is dazzling!" Yet others proclaim things like, "What an ingenious Creator to have designed all of this!" and "The Lord sure has made some beautiful animals." Then suddenly the thought dawns on you: "These folks sound like they live in different worlds."

This fanciful thought experiment is intended to illustrate how different scientific paradigms fundamentally influence our experience, *even when we think we are plainly observing, not interpreting, what is around us*. Thomas Kuhn put it this way when discussing the different perspectives of scientists devoted to competing paradigms:

> Practicing in different worlds, the two groups of scientists see different things when they look from the same point in the same direction. Again, that is not to say that they can see anything they please. Both are looking at the world, and what they look at has not changed. But in some areas they see different things, and they see them in different relations one to the other. That is why a law that cannot even be

demonstrated to one group of scientists may occasionally seem intuitively obvious to another. Equally, it is why, before they can hope to communicate fully, one group or the other must experience the conversion that we have been calling a paradigm shift. Just because it is a transition between incommensurables, the transition between competing paradigms cannot be made a step at a time, forced by logic and neutral experience. Like the gestalt switch, it must occur all at once (though not necessarily in an instant) or not at all.[5]

Another scientist-turned-philosopher, chemist Michael Polanyi, actually predated Kuhn in arguing for some of the same ideas. Like Kuhn, Polanyi critiqued the notion of scientific objectivity, emphasized the interpretive role of theories, and even used some of the same imagery as Kuhn in articulating his ideas: "Scientists—that is, creative scientists—spend their lives in trying to guess right. They are sustained and guided therein by their heuristic passion. We call their work creative because it changes the world as we see it, by deepening our understanding of it. . . . Having made the discovery, I shall never see the world as before. My eyes have become different."[6]

A major theme in Polanyi's work is the notion that all scientific research and theorizing is *personal*, rather than a strictly mechanical process. Scientists bring biases, desires, and passionate commitments to their work just like anyone else. So he agrees with Kuhn's observation that a shift in theoretical perspective "cannot be . . . forced by logic." The personal concerns of scientists sometimes override the pure implications of data, and theories are often selected or defended on this basis rather than just empirical evidence or logical reasoning.

Many Kuhnians have noted how non-rational factors influence the rise and fall of paradigms, including psychological factors (e.g., professional ambition, personal hubris, etc.) and sociological factors (e.g., community needs, industrial pressures, etc.).[7] Philosopher of science Paul Feyerabend even goes so far as to argue that theory selection in science is essentially subjective. Since paradigms are incommensurable and objectivity is impossible, "what remains . . . are aesthetic judgments, judgments of taste, metaphysical prejudices, religious desires, in short, *what remains are our subjective wishes.*"[8] Most would agree that Feyerabend goes too far in taking a subjectivist view of science. But that psychological and sociological factors have influenced the growth and preservation of paradigms is undeniable, as history shows. I would say that role is especially significant today, given the hugely expanded influence of business, government, and public opinion on scientific enterprise.

While I am no postmodernist, and frankly consider the postmodern denial of objective truth to be incoherent, I do think Kuhn's main points are on the mark when it comes to science. All scientific observation is to some extent interpreted through a paradigm. However neutral he or she might pretend to be, the scientist always filters data through a set of unspoken (or unconscious) presuppositions. And if this is true regarding science, then how much more so for the rest of us, whether we are mechanics, marketers, farmers, or philosophers. We all subscribe to any number of paradigms, including models for understanding history (e.g., linear or cyclical, purposeful or random); politics (e.g., monarchy, democracy, republic); economics (e.g., socialism, capitalism, welfare liberalism); psychology (e.g., behaviorism, cognitivism, Freudian psychoanalysis); general worldview (e.g., theism, pantheism, atheism); and theology (e.g., Catholic, Protestant, Sunni, Shiite). Our paradigms fundamentally condition the way we perceive events and process ideas and arguments. This explains why we all tend to become entrenched in our views and why it is so rare that scholars experience wholesale worldview changes in the middle of their careers. As someone once put it, scholars tend to suffer "hardening of the categories," and this is true of laypersons as well.

So how might these Kuhnian insights aid us in understanding atheists? For one thing, the atheistic paradigm has its own standards for truth, many of which pivot on their naturalist conviction that only the physical world exists. Necessarily, they will reject as false and perhaps even as irrational nonsense all references to miracles, souls, divine authority of Scripture, or personal experience of God. It is difficult for theists to reason with atheists about worldview matters when such basic features of the spiritual life are so denigrated. For this reason, we should not expect atheists to respond positively to rational arguments. While some, such as C. S. Lewis and Antony Flew, eventually do experience the gestalt switch to theism—where arguments even appear to have played a decisive role—these are rare exceptions to the rule. In most cases, we can expect our most cogent arguments to fall on deaf ears. I will hasten to add that, nonetheless, we should "always be prepared to give an answer to everyone who asks you to give the reason for the hope that you have" (1 Peter 3:15). It is our Christian duty to be schooled in the evidences for the faith.

Second, theists and atheists do, in a sense, live in different worlds. God is at the center of the theist's worldview, and this colors his or her every experience and value judgment. On the other hand, the axis of a worldview without God is necessarily the self, and the atheist's values and personal experience are shaped accordingly. It is no wonder that we find the "two worlds" distinction made so emphatically in Scripture. Jesus declares, "My kingdom is not of this world" (John 18:36). Paul repeatedly distinguishes gospel values and "the basic principles of this world" (Galatians 4:3; Colossians 2:8; 20). Peter calls Christians "aliens and strangers in the world" (1 Peter 2:11). And John says those who are not from God "speak from the viewpoint of the world" (1 John 4:5).[9] The difference in perspective is compounded when we consider the concept of spiritual discernment, which is granted only to those in whom the Holy Spirit dwells. As Paul writes, "The man without the Spirit does not accept the things that come from the Spirit of God, for they are foolishness to him, and he cannot understand them, because they are spiritually discerned" (1 Corinthians 2:14). So, if these biblical teachings are true, then we should *expect* to see dramatic differences of perspective between atheists and theists. And the gulf should be especially pronounced between atheists and Christians, whose paradigms are, one might say, supernaturally reinforced.

Those who see the world through the lens of a false or distorting paradigm suffer from what I call *paradigm-induced blindness*. Their theoretical framework prevents them from seeing the truth, even when it is right in front of them. In a sense this condition is more pernicious than simple ignorance, because the person labors under the illusion of enlightenment and clear-sightedness. He or she is always ready to pontificate on the stubbornness or academic foolishness of others who do not "see" so clearly as they. When one's worldview is naturalism, paradigm-induced blindness naturally prevents one from seeing certain sinful practices as immoral, particularly in the sexual sphere. And those who affirm Christian sexual standards will necessarily appear foolish or absurd to the atheist. In turn, their incredulity and repugnance regarding the "narrow" or "repressed" Christian sexual ethic serve to reinforce their will to disbelieve and further entrench them in the atheist paradigm.

A third application regards the factors that influence paradigm shifts. According to Kuhn, many of the determining factors are non-rational in nature, ranging from psychological dispositions to sociological influences. This insight dovetails well with the biblical diagnosis of atheism. We have already discussed some of the fallout of a defective father relationship and chronic immoral behavior when it comes to belief in God. The combination of these factors appears to predispose a person to embrace an atheistic paradigm. Put another way, the moral and emotional damage resulting from these dynamics opens the door to atheism that might otherwise remain psychologically closed. However, as we have also noted, these factors are not sufficient by themselves to bring about the paradigm shift to atheism. A person's *will* must assert itself, voluntarily rejecting God, perhaps explicitly but more likely implicitly through God-defying attitudes such as resentment, unforgiveness, and hatred as well as through other ongoing immoral indulgences. Then, after a period of time, a person finds himself or herself in a state of genuine disbelief regarding God, and the gestalt switch from theism to atheism is complete. The switch is not made quickly or easily, however (as confirmed by the overwhelming majority of theists). There are moral-psychological reasons for this, which we will explore in the next section.

TRUTH OR CONSEQUENCES

In Jane Austen's *Emma*, the novel's namesake is very bright but too sure of her own opinions, even to the point of refusing to allow evidence to change her mind. Some of Emma's friends, including one Mr. Knightley, are exasperated by her obstinacy. One day while discussing the romantic interests of a mutual friend, Knightley rebukes her, saying, "Better be without sense, than misapply it as you do."[10]

Mr. Knightley's point applies well to the topic at hand. When used properly, human reason is a profound gift, blessing us with everything from love sonnets to GPS technology. But when abused, few things wreak as much destruction. In fact, the greatest evils in human history have involved diabolical genius. What landed men like Herod, Ivan the Terrible, and Adolf Hitler in the annals of the wicked was not lack of reason but the clever pursuit of the wrong ends. Their problem was not bad logic but "misapplying" it to faulty presuppositions—mistaken views about such things as the sanctity of human life and the proper role of government. It is a safe bet that on judgment day it will be better to have lived as a foolish ignoramus than one of these ingenious despots.

So, as important as reasoning ability is, what is most decisive in human affairs is *truth*. This is especially the case when it comes to the reality of God, the most fundamental of all truths. Fortunately for us, God has made His presence obvious. As Paul declares, God's existence and attributes are clear from what has been made so that no one has an excuse not to believe (Romans 1:20). Now this raises the question *Why?* Is it that the evidence for God is so clear that any reasonable person should *infer* that God exists and has certain qualities? While this might be so, some theologians have suggested that there is a deeper, psychological reason for this. For example, the great Protestant reformer John Calvin contended: "There is within the human mind, and indeed by natural instinct, an awareness of divinity. This we take to be beyond controversy. To prevent anyone from taking refuge in the pretense of ignorance, God himself has implanted in all men a certain understanding of his divine majesty."[11] Elsewhere he says,

> Men of sound judgment will always be sure that a sense of divinity which can never be effaced is engraved upon men's minds. Indeed, the perversity of the impious, who though they struggle furiously are unable to extricate themselves from the fear of God, is abundant testimony that this conviction, namely,

that there is some God, is naturally inborn in all, and is fixed deep within, as it were in the very marrow.[12]

This sense of the divine, or *sensus divinitatis*, Calvin also calls the "seed of religion."[13] Let's highlight a few points about it. First, on Calvin's account, the sense of the divine is universal. All human beings are blessed with this awareness, which helps to explain Paul's insistence that, in reflecting on God's created works, no one has an excuse not to believe. Consequently, the most one can do is "struggle furiously" against the awareness of God and the fear it evokes. However, if the *sensus divinitatis* is universal and cannot be completely squelched, then how can there be atheists? The answer is actually simple. To deny the reality of God is not inconsistent with some level of awareness of God. Recall Paul's phrase that the wicked "suppress" the truth of God (Romans 1:18). This suggests that although the sense of the divine can be diminished, it can never be totally eradicated. To use a computer analogy, one might compare the *sensus divinitatis* to an operating system that is coded into the hard drive. A human being can no more purge her awareness of God than a computer can remove its operating system.

Second, on Calvin's account the awareness of God is natural in the sense that it is inborn or innate. As he expresses it, the *sensus divinitatis* is "engraved" or "implanted" in all human minds. Somehow, each of us comes into this world equipped with what we might call a spiritual "antenna," to use yet another analogy. As one matures, this antenna becomes operational, usually beginning in early childhood. Many parents, like myself, can attest to the natural ability in children to understand and respond to the reality of God.[14] However, the *sensus divinitatis* should not be confused with a formal idea or concept of God. To be "aware" of something, one need not be capable of articulating or defining the object of that awareness. So it goes with the *sensus divinitatis*. Even small children have a sense of the divine, even if they lack the linguistic or conceptual tools to effectively communicate this.

Third, the *sensus divinitatis*, according to Calvin, has a cognitive component. In his words, we all are endowed with "a certain understanding of . . . divine majesty." Our sense of the divine is intellectually active, naturally leading to the formation of beliefs about God, such as regards His power, wisdom, knowledge, and goodness. It also gives rise to various beliefs about right and wrong, as the *sensus divinitatis* is closely related to conscience, which is a moral response to this awareness of God. The concept of conscience has a biblical foundation, such as where Paul asserts, "When Gentiles, who do not have the law, do by nature things required by the law, they are a law for themselves, even though they do not have the law, since they show that the requirements of the law are written on their hearts, their consciences also bearing witness, and their thoughts now accusing, now even defending them" (Romans 2:14–15). Calvin's notion of the *sensus divinitatis* seems to capture or include these things.[15]

The concept of the *sensus divinitatis* is helpful in several respects. For one thing, it provides insight into the psychology of theistic belief-formation, as many theists, Christians and otherwise, will readily attest. This, in turn, helps to account for the widespread belief in God, even in the absence of formal religion. But the *sensus divinitatis* has explanatory power on the negative side as well, enabling us to better understand the phenomenon of atheism. To show exactly how this is so, it will be necessary to discuss the impact of sin on the mind. And to do this I would like to draw again from the work of Alvin Plantinga.

In an earlier chapter we noted how naturalism undermines itself. Specifically, we saw how Plantinga shows that a worldview cannot be rational unless it can somehow account for the reliability of human cognition in producing true beliefs. If a worldview, such as naturalism, gives us no reason to think that our belief-forming mechanisms are generally trustworthy, then we have no reason to believe that worldview is *true*. Nor, given that worldview, should we trust any other beliefs that we happen to hold.[16]

To the chagrin of naturalists, only theism holds the solution to this problem. Here is the gist of Plantinga's argument. (Quickly summarizing 980 pages of scholarly argumentation is a bit of a challenge, but I'll give it a shot.) To call a cognitive system *reliable* presupposes the notion of a purpose or goal at which one's rational faculties aim. That purpose is the acquisition of truth. Our rational faculties are generally reliable only if they can be counted on to produce a preponderance of true rather than false beliefs. Another way of putting this is to say that the *function* of human cognition is to produce true beliefs. And our cognitive processes are trustworthy only when they are functioning properly.

To say that human cognition functions for a purpose suggests that it was *designed*. As Plantinga notes, the notion of proper function "is inextricably bound with another: that of a *design plan*. Human beings and their organs are so constructed that there is a way that they *should* work, a way they are *supposed* to work, a way they work when they work right."[17] Most naturalists, of course, find this appalling. Nothing is more anathema to atheism than the concept of design (well, except for the concept of God).[18] But there really is no getting around Plantinga's point. If you want to salvage any sense of reliability in human cognition, you have to admit design (in order to make sense of cognitive purpose and proper function, which in turn make sense of cognitive reliability).

Of course, human cognition does not always function properly. Like any system that is designed to function a certain way, our cognitive system may malfunction, particularly when hampered in some way. Plantinga writes,

> Many systems of your body, obviously, are designed to work in a certain kind of environment. You can't breathe under water; your muscles atrophy in zero gravity; you can't get enough oxygen at the top of Mount Everest. Clearly, the same goes for your cognitive faculties; they too will achieve their purpose only if functioning in an environment much like the one for which they were designed.[19]

Now this notion of cognitive malfunction has particular application to our awareness of God: "There is such a thing as cognitive disease; there is blindness, deafness, inability to tell right from wrong, insanity; and there are analogues of these conditions with respect to the operation of the *sensus divinitatis*."[20] Thus, when it comes to atheism, Plantinga concludes, "It is really the unbeliever who displays epistemic malfunction; failing to believe in God is a result of some kind of dysfunction of the *sensus divinitatis*."[21]

What causes malfunction in any system always comes back to the fall. Sin and its consequences have wreaked havoc on the world, and human cognition is no exception. In short, sin disrupts our ability to think straight. Theologians call this the "noetic effects of sin." To return to the computer analogy, as part of the "operating system" of the human mind, damage to the *sensus divinitatis* will negatively affect human cognition, impacting many mental functions in addition to our thoughts about God. For instance, such damage will necessarily corrupt our thinking about ethics, human nature, purpose in history, and origins, to name just a few topics. Discussion of such issues is outside the scope of this book, but it is worth noting that the noetic effects of sin extend far beyond theological matters. Cognition about God is only the most immediately impacted by sin.

THE PSYCHOLOGY OF SELF-DECEPTION

In our discussion of Kuhn's philosophy of science, we noted that non-rational factors influence paradigm choice. The studies by Johnson and Jones vividly illustrate a disturbing example of this—the desire for sexual freedom. The most natural paradigm of choice for rationalizing one's sexual misbehavior is ethical relativism, since this perspective denies that there are any moral absolutes, even regarding sexual conduct. And it is not surprising that scholars who embrace this paradigm would also devote their intellectual energy to defending it, even at the expense of academic integrity.

To combine Kuhn's insights with those of Johnson and Jones, many of the intellectuals discussed in the previous chapter were committed to paradigms that blinded them. But their embracing of these paradigms was spawned and reinforced by their own immoral behavior and refusal to change or admit they were doing wrong. Their preference for the relativist, and in many cases atheist, paradigms they chose and defended amounted to a concerted *will to disbelieve* when it came to the moral law and the God in whom it originates. I offer this analysis as a model for understanding the moral psychology involved in those who "suppress the truth by their wickedness" (Romans 1:18). To draw some other dynamics we have discussed into this summary, the paradigm of moral relativism and the will to disbelieve both contribute to a dampening of the *sensus divinitatis* and general cognitive malfunction, especially regarding moral and spiritual matters. This in turn opens the door to even more perverse and shameless behavior. And so goes the cycle of rebellion and disbelief.

One might say that this entire causal pattern, as expressed in the model I am proposing here, can be conceived as the psychological machinery of *self-deception*. Indeed, many theists have described atheists as self-deceived, but I have endeavored here to unpack the causal dynamics involved. If the atheist really is self-deceived, then the model I have proposed aims to explain what this *means*.

Self-deception is a much-debated psychological concept, and in researching for my book on the subject of hypocrisy,[22] I learned how complex and even mystifying it is. The phenomenon has been variously analyzed in terms of lying to oneself, motivated irrationality, conflicting subconscious processes, and existential disavowal, to name a few theories. But the essential feature of self-deception is a denial of what, at some level, one knows to be true. If the *sensus divinitatis* can never be completely expunged, then anyone who disbelieves in God's existence denies what, at some level, he or she knows to be true. This does seem to be a case of self-deception, if anything is.

Clearly, many of the modern intellectuals discussed above were motivated by sexual liberation, as Aldous Huxley freely admitted. This is a morally pernicious brand of self-deception, since the *motives* are themselves immoral. Irrational devotion to a paradigm may be irresponsible and even exasperating, but it is quite a different matter to remain obstinately committed to a paradigm that rejects morality itself so that one can pursue vice in a guilt-free way. No wonder that in judgment of this the source of morality Himself would deliver such people to depravity (Romans 1:24–32).

My account of atheism is now complete, and I have reviewed some of the main elements above. But I would like to close this chapter with a more succinct summary:

The *descent* into atheism is caused by a complex of moral-psychological factors, not a perceived lack of evidence for God's existence. The atheist willfully rejects God, though this is precipitated by immoral indulgences and typically a broken relationship with his or her father. Thus, the choice of the atheistic paradigm is motivated by non-rational factors, some of which are psychological and some of which are moral in nature.

The *hardening* of the atheistic mind-set occurs through cognitive malfunction due to two principal causes. First, atheists suffer from paradigm-induced blindness, as their worldview inhibits their ability to recognize the reality of God that is manifest in creation. Second, atheists suffer from damage to the *sensus divinitatis*, so their natural awareness of God is severely impeded. Both of these mechanisms are aspects of the noetic effects of sin.

This combination of factors amounts to a deadly cognitive cocktail when it comes to religious belief. However, thankfully, even the atheist is not beyond reach of the redemptive power of God. In the final chapter we will look at some of the cognitive benefits of commitment to God and how faith can be intentionally nurtured. We will see how, relative to atheism, the way of faith is like living in a different world.

5

THE BLESSINGS
OF THEISM

IN DECEMBER 2008 an article appeared in the *Times Online* with this arresting title: "As an Atheist, I Truly Believe Africa Needs God." The journalist was foreign correspondent and award-winning author Matthew Parris. Having lived in several African countries early in his life, Parris was intimately familiar with the continent and the depth of its problems, both social and economic. So when he returned to his native land after more than four decades away, he was struck by the developmental work being carried on by Christian mission organizations. And he finally allowed himself to admit something he'd been resisting all of these years:

> Now a confirmed atheist, I've become convinced of the enormous contribution that Christian evangelism

makes in Africa: sharply distinct from the work of secular NGOs, government projects and international aid efforts. These alone will not do. Education and training alone will not do. In Africa Christianity changes people's hearts. It brings a spiritual transformation. The rebirth is real. The change is good.

I used to avoid this truth by applauding—as you can—the practical work of mission churches in Africa. It's a pity, I would say, that salvation is part of the package, but Christians black and white, working in Africa, do heal the sick, do teach people to read and write; and only the severest kind of secularist could see a mission hospital or school and say the world would be better without it.[1]

Parris goes on to describe the differences he has observed among African Christians, noting how they seemed more relaxed, lively, and curious than non-converts and that they had "an engagement with the world . . . that seemed to be missing in traditional African life."

Although Parris appears to remain firm in his atheism, one can only wonder to what extent this experience might soften his heart toward Christianity and theism generally. The point is that there is apologetic power in a life well-lived. As it was in the early church, when Christians won converts by simply demonstrating their love for one another, so it is today. Personal virtue and self-sacrifice are the most effective tools of persuasion, able to overcome gargantuan obstacles of doubt and lure even the most skeptical minds. When it comes to proving religious truth, an ounce of love is worth a ton of argument.

CHRISTIAN VIRTUE AND COGNITIVE HEALTH

So virtue is a powerful apologetic for unbelievers. This is perhaps an obvious truth. What is less obvious, but no less important for the church, is the fact that virtue is also crucial for the preservation of faith for those who already believe. There are several reasons for this. For one thing, by living virtuously one avoids the negative effects of vice—the deadening of the *sensus divinitatus* and various aspects of cognitive corruption discussed earlier, such as self-deception and paradigm-induced blindness. The less one's cognitive system is damaged, the better it can fulfill its function to produce true beliefs. Therefore, the more virtuously one lives, the more truth one is able to access, including truths about God and how to obey Him. As the psalmist says, "The statutes of the Lord are trustworthy, making wise the simple" (Psalm 19:7).[2] And, of course, right belief issuing forth in righteous conduct constitutes the essence of biblical faith.

An important point here is that given the truth of theism, any benefit for human cognition is also a boon to religious belief. If God is real, then whatever helps the mind to grasp reality will also support faith in

God. In light of this, another way that virtuous living helps cognition and, in turn, theistic belief is by preventing motives for willful disbelief. A vicious or immoral person has a motive to reject vital truths that condemn his or her lifestyle. So the less vice in one's life, the fewer ulterior motives one will have to disbelieve such truths, whether they concern ethics or the reality of God. Put another way, one's sinful commitments cause cognitive interference by the will, so the more virtuous person will be less susceptible to such interference. All of these considerations confirm E. Michael Jones's insight that "the intellectual life is a function of the moral life of the thinker. In order to apprehend truth, which is the goal of the intellectual life, one must live a moral life."[3]

There is yet another way in which right living may improve cognition. To understand this, let's return to the concept of a paradigm. Earlier we noted how false paradigms can so impair a person's ability to properly interpret experience that they blind one to obvious truths. There is also a considerable upside to paradigms when they are true or at least approximately true. They have the power to enlighten, to clarify and sharpen one's experience of the world. The theistic worldview is, of course, a particular paradigm. As a theist, naturally, I believe it is a *true* paradigm, the most accurate and enlightening of all worldviews. If this is so, then any behavior that reinforces or enriches this paradigm will, in turn, enlighten me and improve my perception of the world.

With this in mind, consider the apostle Paul's exhortation to dwell on "anything . . . excellent or praiseworthy" (Philippians 4:8). One significant category of excellence is nature's beauty, from rainbows and mountain ranges to jellyfish and hummingbirds. As we contemplate the aesthetic excellence of the world, this prompts us to consider God as the creative source of all things. Reflection on the beauty of creation naturally stimulates reflection on the creative Artist behind it. This reinforces a theistic paradigm and the inclination to see God as the central reality. And, as noted above, if theism is true, then this reinforcement will improve one's understanding and perception of the world (for example, to better appreciate God's artistry in creation). In short, obedience—in this case, to the command to reflect on aesthetic excellence—improves cognition. And, again, given the truth of theism, whatever improves cognition is good for faith.

This general point about the influence of behavior on cognitive health suggests some practical applications. For one thing, we must keep in mind that our reading and entertainment habits affect the way we think about the world, so we must be critically aware of these aspects of our lives. And it is wise to intentionally nourish one's theological paradigm by reading good books and engaging in informative dialogue.[4] Also, all of this places a premium on spiritual formation and the practice of the spiritual disciplines. The study of Scripture and singing of hymns directly impact our cognitive processes, of course. But fasting, sacrifice, and other practices of self-denial build self-control, which enables a person to better resist all sorts of temptations.[5] This translates into a reduction of sin in one's life, and for the reasons just explained, this will bring cognitive benefits, including insights into theological truth. So while such disciplines as worship, study, meditation, and fellowship tend to build faith directly, such disciplines as fasting, solitude, service, frugality, and sacrifice build faith indirectly.[6]

The Right to Complain and the Privilege to Thank

It is often noted, both by scholars and laypeople, that the life of faith brings many emotional benefits, including relief from the burden of guilt for one's sins and the hope for a joyous eternal life after death. There are many other such benefits less frequently recognized, perhaps because they are not as momentous. But they are worth noting, both because they are psychologically satisfying and they contribute to the growth and preservation of faith. One of these is the *right to express our complaints to God*. As people of prayer, all theists speak to God. In addition to praising God and making requests, we may complain to Him about things that disturb or harm us.

Regardless of one's beliefs about God, we all recognize the right to complain about the rude or unjust actions of another person. This is sometimes an appropriate thing to do, provided it is done in a responsible way. (I take a "just" complaint to be an expression of dissatisfaction about some wrongful action directed to a culpable party.) Thus, we enjoy the right to complain about bad service at a restaurant or a neighbor who plays music loudly late into the night. Even a civil lawsuit for some harm can be seen as a form of complaint. But what of unpleasant or harmful occurrences that have no human cause or where there is no means available to address the person responsible? To whom may one complain when diagnosed with pancreatic cancer or when one's home is destroyed by an earthquake or tornado? What complaint can be issued when a foreign nation attacks your homeland and brutalizes your family and friends?

For the atheist, complaints of any kind are useless and even absurd in such circumstances. Malignancies and natural disasters "just happen"—they are the cards that "nature" deals you, and you simply have to accept them and move on as best you can. Similarly, in the face of overwhelmingly powerful enemies, complaints are useless or counterproductive. In contrast, in these cases the theist does have a right to complain—*to God*. The Lord is sovereign over the workings of nature, down to every cell in our bodies (cf. Colossians 1:17; Hebrews 1:3a). Rulers and governments only exercise the power God allows (cf. Romans 13:1;

1 Peter 2:13). And God has specific plans for all those who love Him (cf. Psalm 139:13–16; Romans 8:28). So there are no events that fall outside the divine jurisdiction and, therefore, no undeserved harms about which we may not take our grievance to God.

The Psalms provide numerous examples of such complaints:

How long, O Lord? Will you forget me forever? How long will you hide your face from me? How long must I wrestle with my thoughts and every day have sorrow in my heart? How long will my enemy triumph over me? (Psalm 13:1–2)

You have made us a reproach to our neighbors, the scorn and derision of those around us. You have made us a byword among the nations; the peoples shake their heads at us. . . . All this happened to us, though we had not forgotten you or been false to your covenant. . . . Yet for your sake we face death all day long; we are considered as sheep to be slaughtered. Awake, O Lord! Why do you sleep? Rouse yourself! Do not reject us forever. Why do you hide your face and forget our misery and oppression? (Psalm 44:13–14, 17, 22–24)

These and many other "bluesy" psalms[7] issue protests to God for His seeming apathy or injustice regarding human suffering. They reassure us that we may freely act on the impulse to complain to God, to "get it off our chest," as we consider our plight or the sorrows of those we love. The right to complain must be exercised because it will prevent bitterness and resentment toward God in our struggle with the practical problem of evil. These negative emotions are sometimes the first steps toward doubt and, ultimately, disbelief. I have never known an atheist, agnostic, or "ex-Christian" who did not have some harrowing personal experience that crushed him or her emotionally.

On the other end of the spectrum of fortune are blessings. As with complaints, all of us enjoy the freedom to thank other people for the ways they help us. But what of the "natural" blessings we enjoy? Whom do we thank for our good health, intelligence, and innate physical and artistic talents? Again, the atheist can only point to eons of blind evolutionary forces that have culminated in endowing us so richly. Or what of nature itself in all its resplendent beauty? Whom can we praise for it? A former pastor of mine used to tell the story of an agnostic zoologist who would go on and on about the extraordinary splendor of organisms he studied. He just couldn't get over the wonder of it all, my pastor explained: "It was almost as if he wanted someone to thank."[8] Indeed, we all do. As believers, we must take advantage of this *privilege to thank and praise God*, and we should do so often.

Many psalms effusively praise God for the wonders of creation:

> The heavens declare the glory of God; the skies proclaim the work of his hands. Day after day they pour forth speech; night after night they display knowledge. (Psalm 19:1–2)

> When I consider your heavens, the work of your fingers, the moon and the stars, which you have set in place, what is man that you are mindful of him, the son of man that you care for him? (Psalm 8:3–4)

> I praise you because I am fearfully and wonderfully made; your works are wonderful, I know that full well. (Psalm 139:14)

There is something about excellence of any kind that motivates us to praise. When you hear a great song, see an outstanding athletic play, or read a superb book, you want to extol its excellence and tell others about it. If this is the case with human accomplishments, then how much more so with those things that far surpass human creation? From the dynamic intricacy of a single living cell to the mind-boggling immensity of a galaxy—or, for that matter, the hundreds of billions of galaxies that make up our universe—every aspect of the cosmos displays a certain excellence and warrants praise. No wonder most people do erupt in praise of the Creator, even when they know little about whom it is they praise. For the atheist, however, this impulse is frustrated. Their worldview does not permit them this privilege.

Offering thanks and praise to God can be profoundly satisfying as a form of psychological release. It feels good to "tell it like it is," especially when the things we acknowledge God for are ingenious and astounding. Also, the privilege to thank should be acted upon because it is the just and right thing to do. Atheist David Hume once declared that ingratitude is the worst of vices, and this might not be far from the truth, especially considering the role of ingratitude in the Romans 1 pattern for descent into atheism (see Romans 1:21). The failure to be adequately appreciative can distort one's perception of reality, particularly regarding one's sense of pride and autonomy. In contrast, the more we give thanks, the more we become aware of our dependence and further blessings for which to be thankful. So showing gratitude to God increases awareness and insight into divine goodness and makes us more humble and eager to obey. This has further salutary effects on the mind as noted above. Call it the virtuous cycle of virtue and wisdom: virtue begets wisdom, and wisdom begets virtue. All of this shows that we should take advantage of the privilege to thank and praise God. It satisfies emotionally and fertilizes faith.[9]

THERE BUT FOR GRACE . . .

Matthew Parris is right. Christianity is good for us. Even though, as an atheist, Parris would deny that it really is Jesus Christ who is responsible for the changes he sees in Africans, he can't deny the reality of those changes, nor the goodness of the work being done by Christian missionaries to bring about those changes. But it *is* God in Christ who brings this redemption. These Christians have taken initiative to address personal and social needs, but they do so in response to the redemption they've experienced and by the power of the One who works in them. They simply aim to pay forward what God has graciously given them. So it goes for any real Christian. We are spiritual beneficiaries who would like to see others benefit as well.

Some of us take awhile before coming on board. I used to be Malcolm Crowe. I was a ghost who didn't know he was dead. Before I was a Christian, I lived a wicked life, suppressing the truth of God that I knew but was unwilling to acknowledge. As I recall the narrative of my conversion as a young man, there are many junctures at which divine intervention occurred. But what I can't understand is why He so intervened, for I did nothing to deserve it. In fact, everything I did warranted God's judgment, not His mercy. I reached out to God only when He had taken hold of me. He awakened me to my deadness, even as He made me alive. The Lover of my soul loved me and so enabled me to love Him back and to extend that same love to others, though always imperfectly and often in a fumbling sort of way.

As Christians, we need to demonstrate our love for God, as an encouragement and as a testimony of faith both to believers and unbelievers. This love is not solely a matter of affection, though it certainly includes that. It is also, perhaps most importantly, a matter of virtue. As the apostle Paul makes clear, to love is to display *goodness* toward someone, in the form of virtues such as patience, kindness, humility, courtesy, forgiveness, truthfulness, trust, and perseverance (1 Corinthians 13:4–7). This is the first and last order of business for any Christian, whether one is a scholar or a layperson. And if we improve in this area, then we will improve in all areas, especially in making the case for God and Christian truth.

Let's not give atheists moral ammunition for their skeptical cannons. Let's demonstrate patience and long-suffering with them. Let's affirm them where they are correct (e.g., on church hypocrisy and the problem of evil). Let's open our minds to their truth claims and interests as much as possible, whether concerning science, art, politics, or anything else. And where we cannot agree, let's resolve to listen anyway and give them the last word or paragraph, even when they are angry, rude, unfair, or belligerent. Let's remember that they live with pains and disappointments as much as the rest of us, if not more so. Let's not forget that they might see us "religious" folk as the enemy because we represent the same theological beliefs and moral ideals as those who have treated them maliciously in the past. Let's be willing to be shortchanged, belittled, ridiculed, and scorned, and not return the same. In short, let's live the Golden Rule as effectively as we can in their midst and not just because it might persuade them to believe, but because it's the right thing to do. After all, that's how Jesus did it.

ACKNOWLEDGMENTS

THIS BOOK WAS as challenging as it was enlightening to write, and I have benefited from the help of many people along the way.

The folks at Moody Publishers have been wonderful partners in this project. Thanks especially to Madison Trammel, both for his sage editorial guidance and his unwavering confidence in the book's bold thesis. I owe a similar debt to Chris Reese, whose stylistic and conceptual fine-tuning has improved every page. It has been a pleasure and a privilege to work with such pros.

Thanks also to Andrew Wolgemuth and everyone else at Wolgemuth and Associates, Inc. They shared my vision for this book from the start, and Andrew's input along the way was invaluable. I also benefited tremendously from Philip Byers's keen editorial eye and generous spirit. And I want to thank my pastor Bob O'Bannon, my good friend Dan Newcomb, and my brother Robert Spiegel for their steadfast support during all phases of this project.

I remain indebted to two Christian communi-ties—New Life Presbyterian Church in Yorktown, Indiana, and Taylor University, especially my fine col-leagues in the Department of Biblical Studies, Chris-tian Education, and Philosophy.

Finally, I thank my wife, Amy, and our children, Bailey, Samuel, Magdalene, and Andrew, for their love, inspiration, and constant encouragement.

Thanks to all of these beautiful people and, above all, to the God who made them—in whom we live and move and have our being.

NOTES

Introduction

1. Christopher Hitchens, *God Is Not Great* (New York: Twelve Books, 2007), 13.

2. Sam Harris, *Letter to a Christian Nation* (New York: Random House), 55–56.

3. Richard Dawkins, *The God Delusion* (New York: Houghton Mifflin, 2006), 51.

4. See Timothy Keller, *The Reason for God* (New York: Dutton, 2008); Alister McGrath and Joanna C. McGrath, *The Dawkins Delusion?* (Downers Grove, IL: InterVarsity, 2007); Ravi Zacharias, *The End of Reason* (Grand Rapids: Zondervan, 2008); and David Berlinski, *The Devil's Delusion* (New York: Crown Forum, 2008).

5. Thomas Nagel, *The Last Word* (New York: Oxford University Press, 1997), 130.

6. National Public Radio interview with Richard Dawkins on "Fresh Air" (March 28, 2007), available on NPR website: http://www.npr.org/templates/player/mediaPlayer.html?action=1&t=1&islist=false&id=9180871&m=9180876.

7. See Alvin Plantinga, *Warranted Christian Belief* (Oxford: Oxford University Press, 2000), chapter 7.

Chapter 1: Atheistic Arguments, Errors, and Insights

1. "Atheists Plan Anti-God Ad Campaign on Buses," Associated Press, October 23, 2008.

2. Ibid.

3. " 'Why Believe in a God? Just Be Good' Ads Set to Run Next Week on D.C. Buses," Associated Press, November 11, 2008.

4. Ibid.

5. Antony Flew once distinguished between "positive" and "negative" atheism. A "positive atheist" denotes one who asserts there is no God, while a "negative atheist" describes someone who simply is not a theist. In this book I will use the term "atheism" in Flew's latter sense. See Flew's "The Presumption of Atheism," *Canadian Journal of Philosophy* 2 (1972): 29–53.

6. In taking this approach, I do not mean to question the importance of Christian apologetics. On the contrary, I am a strong believer in the usefulness of evidence to help persuade doubters and confirm the confidence of believers. Besides this, there is also the biblical mandate to be ready with good reasons for one's faith, as is evident in such passages as 1 Peter 3:15 and as is modeled by the apostle Paul in Acts 17. But the point is that belief in God is not *merely* a matter of evidence. There are also personal dynamics, both moral and psychological, that influence belief formation, and it is just such factors with which I am concerned in this book.

7. Fyodor Dostoevsky, *The Brothers Karamazov*, trans. Constance Garnett (New York: William Heinemann, 1945), 224.

8. I believe the free will and greater good theodicies, in tandem, provide a formidable theodicy. For a thorough discussion, see chapter 5 of my book *The Benefits of Providence* (Wheaton, IL: Crossway, 2005). Other excellent resources include Marilyn M. Adams and Robert M. Adams, eds., *The Problem of Evil* (New York: Oxford University Press, 1991) and Peter van Inwagen, ed., *Christian Faith and the Problem of Evil* (Grand Rapids: Eerdmans, 2004).

9. For a good recent presentation of this criticism, see Stewart Goetz and Charles Taliaferro, *Naturalism* (Grand Rapids: Eerdmans, 2008), chapter 4.

10. Richard Dawkins, *River Out of Eden: A Darwinian View of Life* (London: Phoenix Press), 133, emphases mine.

11. Dawkins is inconsistent on this point. Despite his avowed amoralism, he frequently makes moral judgments in his writings. Indeed, one of his recurrent objections to belief in God is essentially a moral complaint—that religion motivates immoral attitudes and behaviors. Dawkins also devotes an entire chapter of *The God Delusion* to account for moral values. Predictably, the best he can do is to offer a form of relativism, where all moral judgments merely reflect cultural preferences. In a telling passage he admits, "It is pretty hard to defend absolutist morals on grounds other than religious ones" (*The God Delusion* [New

York: Houghton Mifflin, 2006], 266). This is precisely the point of the moral objection to atheism, to be discussed later in this chapter.

12. Holmes Rolston III, *Genes, Genesis, and God* (Cambridge: Cambridge University Press, 1999), 161–62.

13. Bertrand Russell, "A Free Man's Worship," in *Why I Am Not a Christian*, ed. Paul Edwards (New York: Simon & Schuster, 1957), 107.

14. Richard Dawkins, as quoted in Henry F. Schaefer, *Science and Christianity: Conflict or Coherence?* (Watkinsville, GA: Apollos Trust, 2003), 134–35.

15. For Kant, the existence of God is actually one of three preconditions for ethics, along with human freedom and the immortality of the soul. Interestingly, atheism can account neither for immortality nor, arguably, human freedom. So, from a Kantian perspective, atheism is an ethical shambles.

16. Friedrich Nietzsche, *The Portable Nietzsche*, trans. Walter Kaufman (New York: Penguin, 1982), 500, emphasis is the author's.

17. Ibid., 501. Emphases are the author's.

18. Sam Harris, *Letter to a Christian Nation* (New York: Random House, 2006), 23.

19. One should keep in mind, of course, that many complaints about "scholarly failure" are warped by the perspective of methodological naturalism, which today dominates the scientific community. Theistic scientists need not feel constrained to avoid all inferences to the supernatural in the context of their research (as methodological naturalists would insist). But my point here is that such inferences may be done more or less responsibly, and many theistic scientists—notably creationists and intelligent design theorists—could do a much better job in this regard.

Chapter 2: The Irrationality of Atheism

1. Associated Press, "Famous Atheist Now Believes in God," December 9, 2004.

2. Flew accomplished this in several works, most notably *God and Philosophy* (New York: Harcourt, Brace, & World, 1966); *The Presumption of Atheism and Other Philosophical Essays on God, Freedom, and Immortality* (New York: Barnes and Noble, 1976); and his most influential essay, "Theology and Falsification," in *New Essays in Philosophical Theology*, ed. Antony Flew and Alasdair

MacIntyre (New York: Macmillan, 1955), 96–99.

3. Antony Flew, *There Is a God: How the World's Most Notorious Atheist Changed His Mind* (New York: HarperCollins, 2007), 93. See also "My Pilgrimage from Atheism to Theism: A Discussion between Antony Flew and Gary Habermas," *Philosophia Christi* 6:2 (2004): 197–211. Available online at http://philchristi.net/library/articles.asp?pid=33&mode=detail.

4. Paul Davies, "Physics and the Mind of God: The Templeton Prize Address," *First Things* 55 (August/September 1995): 32.

5. This does not constitute God-of-the-gaps reasoning, because when it comes to the Big Bang, by definition there could be no physical cause, or at least no scientifically discoverable cause, since what predates the Big Bang is non-physical and beyond the reach of science. That Scripture affirms a beginning to time is evident in such passages as 1 Corinthians 2:7; 2 Timothy 1:9; and Titus 1:2.

6. Metaphysics is the study of what is most real, as opposed to how things appear to us or what can be known through the senses. As a field of study, then, metaphysics is more foundational than science. And in doing scientific inquiry, researchers always bring metaphysical assumptions to their work, regarding such things as the nature of matter, time, causation, essences, and human beings.

7. For an excellent presentation of the cosmic fine-tuning evidence for God, see Robin Collins, "A Scientific Argument for the Existence of God: The Fine-Tuning Design Argument," *Reason for the Hope Within*, ed. Michael J. Murray (Grand Rapids: Eerdmans, 1999), 47–75.

8. Fred Hoyle and C. Wickramasinghe, *Evolution from Space* (New York: Simon & Schuster, 1981), 24.

9. Fred Hoyle, "Hoyle on Evolution," *Nature* 294 (12 November 1981): 105.

10. For a good discussion of the chemical and physical factors that render the primordial soup theory untenable, see Charles B. Thaxton, Walter L. Bradley, and Roger L. Olsen, *The Mystery of Life's Origin: Reassessing Current Theories* (Dallas: Lewis and Stanley, 1992).

11. David J. Chalmers tersely expresses the problem as follows: "The process of natural selection cannot distinguish between me and my zombie twin. Evolution selects properties according to their functional role, and my zombie twin performs all the functions

that I perform just as well as I do; in particular he leaves around just as many copies of his genes. It follows that evolution alone cannot explain why conscious creatures rather than zombies evolved" (from *The Conscious Mind: In Search of a Fundamental Theory* [Oxford: Oxford University Press], 120). For some other good articulations of this problem, see Colin McGinn's *The Mysterious Flame: Conscious Minds in a Material World* (New York: Basic Books, 1999) and John R. Searle, *Mind: A Brief Introduction* (Oxford: Oxford University Press, 2004), chapter 3.

12. An "irreducibly complex" structure or function is one that has many component parts, each of which is crucial for its operation. That is, it could not have been produced incrementally from simpler precursors. Examples range from blood coagulation to sexual reproduction. For good discussions of irreducible complexity, see Michael Behe's *Darwin's Black Box: The Biochemical Challenge to Evolution* (New York: Free Press, 1996), chapters 9–10 and William A. Dembski's *Intelligent Design: The Bridge Between Science and Theology* (Downers Grove, IL: InterVarsity, 1999), chapter 5.

13. My bachelor's degree is in biology, and I affirmed macroevolution for a time. But these and several other issues moved me to the creationist side. Today, a part of me would still *like* to be a full-fledged macroevolutionist—and it is freeing to know that, as a theist, this option remains open to me—but I just don't see it in the data.

14. Christopher Hitchens, *God Is Not Great: How Religion Poisons Everything* (New York: Twelve Books, 2007), 254.

15. Paul's specification of "sensuality" suggests bodily sins, which include not just sexual indiscretions but perhaps also such sins as gluttony, laziness, and violence.

16. In one instance a former fellow believer (and now a former friend, by his own insistence) attacked me viciously for one of my published views (viz., opposition to gay marriage), calling me a "blockhead." I took solace in the fact that this moniker put me in company with Charlie Brown, who, for all his gullibility and hard luck, is a pretty good guy.

17. Søren Kierkegaard, *Works of Love: Some Christian Reflections in the Form of Discourses*, trans. Howard and Edna Hong (New York: Harper and Row, 1962), 11.

18. One might ask how apologetic arguments could ever be useful for atheists, as they were for Lewis and Flew, given that disbelief is occasioned by rebellion. The answer, I think, lies in the fact

that atheists' immoral motivations and firmness of resolve vary widely. Some rebel out of abject pride, while others, as we'll see in later chapters, are driven by a will to avoid shame for perverse conduct. And while some atheists are absolutely resolute in their conviction, others are much less so. A strong theistic argument can aid in humbling a mildly convinced prideful atheist and be used by the Holy Spirit to open his mind to God. Or the Holy Spirit could so work in an atheist's heart that he quits the perverse conduct that occasioned his atheism. Such a person would then be in a position cognitively to perceive and affirm the import of certain evidences for theism. In short, one never knows how the Spirit might alter a person's moral disposition such that it no longer renders the mind impervious to apologetic arguments.

19. See Plantinga's *Warrant and Proper Function* (Oxford: Oxford University Press, 1993), chapter 12. A different version of the same argument appears in his *Warranted Christian Belief* (Oxford: Oxford University Press, 2000), 227–40.

20. By "cognitive system" I mean the combination of physiological and psychological mechanisms that are responsible for mental functions such as belief, judgment, memory, perception, attention, and concept formation.

21. One might say that Plantinga's argument reveals the *logical* futility of atheism, while the apostle Paul describes the *moral-psychological* futility of atheism.

22. G. K. Chesterton, *Orthodoxy* (New York: Doubleday, 1908), 34.

Chapter 3: The Causes of Atheism

1. Interview with Jodie Foster by Dan McLeod, *The Georgia Straight* (July 10–17, 1997): 43.

2. From George Carlin's HBO special, "You Are All Diseased," recorded live at New York City's Beacon Theater (February 6, 1999).

3. Ibid.

4. Not surprisingly, George Carlin majored in philosophy in college, as did many other well-known comedians, including Steve Martin, Dennis Miller, Jay Leno, Joan Rivers, Jimmy Kimmel, and Woody Allen.

5. Paul C. Vitz, *Faith of the Fatherless: The Psychology of Atheism* (Dallas: Spence Publishing, 1999), 3.

6. Ibid., 4, author's emphasis. The first scholar to attempt a psychological deconstruction of theism was Ludwig Feuerbach (1804–1872).

7. Ibid., 13, 16.

8. Freud's concept of an Oedipus complex is notorious for its lack of empirical support. Freud essentially built the theory upon his own personal experience. Although inspired by this theory, Vitz's defective-father hypothesis about atheism does not depend on it or suffer the same evidential difficulties.

9. Vitz, 5.

10. "Christopher Hitchens," Alexander Linklater, *Prospect* (May 2008), http://www.prospectmagazine.co.uk/article_details.php?id=10157.

11. Paul Johnson, *Intellectuals* (New York: Harper and Row, 1988), ix.

12. Aldous Huxley, *Ends and Means: An Inquiry into the Nature of Ideals and into the Methods Employed for Their Realization* (New York: Harper & Bros., 1937), 316.

13. Ibid., 312.

14. E. Michael Jones, *Degenerate Moderns: Modernity as Rationalized Sexual Misbehavior* (San Francisco: Ignatius Press, 1993), 11.

15. Quoted in Ibid., 27–28.

16. Margaret Mead, *Coming of Age in Samoa: A Psychological Study of Primitive Youth for Western Civilization* (New York: Blue Ribbon Books, 1928), 222.

17. See, for example, Jane Howard, *Margaret Mead: A Life* (New York: Simon & Schuster, 1984) and Hilary Lapsley, *Margaret Mead and Ruth Benedict: The Kinship of Women* (Boston: University of Massachusetts Press, 2001).

18. Jones, 37.

19. Specifically, these were two volumes, co-authored with Wardell Pomeroy and others, published under the titles *Sexual Behavior in the Human Male* (1948) and *Sexual Behavior in the Human Female* (1953).

20. Jones, 96.

21. Cornelia Christenson, *Kinsey: A Biography* (Bloomington, IN: Indiana University Press, 1971), 6–7.

22. Ibid., 9.

23. See James H. Jones, *Alfred C. Kinsey: A Public/Private Life* (New York: Norton, 1997) and Jonathan Gathorne-Hardy, *Kinsey: Sex the Measure of All Things* (Bloomington, IN: Indiana University Press, 2004).

24. Jones, *Degenerate Moderns*, 54.

25. Robert Skidelsky, *John Maynard Keynes* (New York: Viking, 1983), 54.

26. John Maynard Keynes, *Two Memoirs: Dr. Melchior, a Defeated Enemy, and My Early Beliefs* (London: Hart-Davis, 1949), 97–98.

27. Jones, *Degenerate Moderns*, 12.

28. William James, *The Varieties of Religious Experience* (New York: Penguin Books, 1958), 424.

29. William James, "The Sentiment of Rationality," *The Will to Believe and Other Essays in Popular Philosophy* (New York: Dover Publications, 1956), 91, 95.

30. William James, "The Will to Believe," *The Will to Believe*, 23.

31. Thomas Nagel, *The Last Word* (New York: Oxford University Press, 1997), 130.

32. Mortimer Adler, *Philosopher at Large* (New York: Macmillan, 1977), 316.

33. Sarah Pulliam, "Blogging the Bible: A Harvard-Educated Reformed Jew Grapples with the Old Testament," *Christianity Today* (April 2009): 64.

Chapter 4: The Obstinacy of Atheism

1. I don't feel guilty about doing this since, after all, you have had more than a decade to see this film!

2. Perhaps in the theologically heterodox world of *The Sixth Sense*, the ghost of Malcolm Crowe does experience some sort of rebirth or renewal. But the film ends before we have a chance to see this, whatever form that might take.

3. Quoted in *Experience of the Sacred*, ed. Sumner B. Twiss and Walter H. Conser Jr. (Hanover, NH: University Press of New England, 1992), 150.

4. The *Star Trek* Spock, not the notorious Freudian child psychologist, Benjamin Spock.

5. Thomas Kuhn, *The Structure of Scientific Revolutions*, 2nd ed. (Chicago: University of Chicago Press, 1970), 150.

6. Michael Polanyi, *Personal Knowledge* (Chicago: University of Chicago Press, 1958), 143.

7. As Kuhn's views matured, he recognized certain independent criteria for paradigm selection, including accuracy, consistency, simplicity, scope, and fruitfulness (*The Essential Tension* [Chicago: University of Chicago Press, 1977], 320–39). Such are necessary, for example, to account for cases in which single experiments are decisive in a paradigm shift, such as the solar eclipse experiment of 1919 that confirmed Einstein's theory.

8. Paul Feyerabend, *Against Method: Outline of an Anarchistic Theory of Knowledge* (London: New Left, 1975), 285. Emphasis is the author's.

9. See also John 17:6–19; Romans 12:2; 1 Corinthians 1:20–28; Ephesians 2:2; 2 Timothy 4:10; James 4:4; 1 John 2:15–17; and 1 John 4:1–4. These and the quoted verses are but a smattering of the dozens of biblical passages that make or assume this important distinction.

10. Jane Austen, *Emma* (New York: Barnes and Noble, 1996), 58.

11. John Calvin, *Institutes of the Christian Religion*, trans. Ford Lewis Battles (Philadelphia: Westminster, 1960), 43.

12. Ibid., 45–46.

13. Thomas Aquinas, too, was sympathetic to this idea, stating, "To know that God exists in a general and confused way is implanted in us by nature" (*Summa Theologica*, vol. 1, trans. English Dominican Fathers [New York: Benziger Brothers, 1947], 12).

14. For studies that confirm and explore the natural spirituality and religious insight of children, see David Hay and Rebecca Nye, *The Spirit of the Child*, rev. ed. (London: Jessica Kingsley, 2006) and Catherine Stonehouse, *Joining Children on the Spiritual Journey: Nurturing a Life of Faith* (Grand Rapids: Baker, 1998).

15. Calvin himself says as much in his commentary on the book of John, where he writes, "There are two principal parts of the light which still remains in corrupt nature: first, the seed of religion is planted in all men; next, the distinction between good and evil is engraved on their consciences" (quoted in Calvin's *Institutes of the Christian Religion*, 43n2).

16. Plantinga's critique of naturalism is actually an aside within a much larger constructive project of developing a distinctively Christian epistemology (theory of knowledge). This decades-long project culminated in a trilogy of books on the nature of knowledge and Christian belief. His work has proven so rich and fruitful

THE MAKING OF AN ATHEIST

that it has impacted scholarly discussions in multiple disciplines, including theology, science, psychology, and education. In his own field of philosophy, the last few decades have seen somewhat of a Christian renaissance, and no one deserves more credit for this than Alvin Plantinga.

17. Alvin Plantinga, *Warranted Christian Belief* (New York: Oxford University Press, 2000), 154, author's emphases.

18. The notion of teleology in nature—the concept that there is purpose in the natural world—is a scandal in most disciplines today, not just the empirical sciences (especially biology) but also the social sciences, history, and even literary criticism. Ironically, the biological taxonomic system, devised by Linnaeus in the eighteenth century, is founded in teleology—the idea that each species has an Aristotelian essence. Thus, the biological classification system itself mocks the reigning Darwinian paradigm, which is fundamentally opposed to essences and all things teleological.

19. Plantinga, *Warranted Christian Belief*, 155.

20. Ibid., 184.

21. Ibid.

22. James Spiegel, *Hypocrisy: Moral Fraud and Other Vices* (Grand Rapids: Baker, 1999), chapter 3.

Chapter 5: The Blessings of Theism

1. Matthew Parris, "As an Atheist, I Truly Believe Africa Needs God," *Times Online* (December 27, 2008): http://www.timeson line.co.uk/tol/comment/columnists/matthew_parris/article54005 68.ece.

2. See also Psalm 25:9 and Proverbs 11:2.

3. E. Michael Jones, *Degenerate Moderns: Modernity as Rationalized Sexual Misbehavior* (San Francisco: Ignatius Press, 1993), 16.

4. I should take care to distinguish a broad or, to use C. S. Lewis's term, "mere" Christian paradigm from the sub-paradigm that is one's Protestant, Catholic, or Orthodox theology, or the sub-sub-paradigm that is one's Reformed, Dispensational, Pentecostal, or Emergent theology. Since the creedal truths of "mere Christianity" (e.g., the existence of God, the virgin birth and resurrection of Jesus Christ, etc.) are the most precious doctrinal truths, they warrant dogmatic affirmation (however harshly the dreaded d-word might fall upon our ears these days). Regarding our theological sub-paradigm and sub-sub-paradigm, we should

constantly examine and reform these beliefs in light of Scripture and sound reasoning.

5. Such practices are examples of the "strict training" for godliness emphasized by Paul in 1 Corinthians 9:24–27 and 1 Timothy 4:7–8.

6. For good resources on the spiritual disciplines, two classic books are Richard Foster's *Celebration of Discipline* (New York: Harper, 1978) and Dallas Willard's *The Spirit of the Disciplines* (San Francisco: HarperCollins, 1988).

7. See also Psalms 22; 59; 64; 74; 88; and 142.

8. I have had a similar reaction when reading certain passages in Richard Dawkins's *The Blind Watchmaker*, where he frequently ponders with awe some organism or biological structure or process.

9. These considerations help to make sense of Paul's seemingly counterintuitive admonition to "give thanks in all circumstances" (1 Thessalonians 5:18).

ISBN-13: 978-0-8024-3194-3

Holly Ordway should never have become a Christian. A young, white, highly educated atheist and professor of English, she represents the kind of person that many observers of religion say cannot be converted anymore—a demographic supposedly beyond the reach of the church in postmodern America. Yet through a series of conversations with a wise and patient friend, Holly not only became convinced of God's existence, but also embraced Jesus as her Savior and Lord. In this memoir of her conversion, she turns her analytical mind toward the path that leads from darkness to light—from death to life. Simultaneously encouraging and bracing, she offers a bold testimony to the ongoing power of the gospel—a gospel that can humble and transform even self-assured, accomplished, and secular-minded young professionals like herself.

HOLLY ORDWAY

MOODY
PUBLISHERS

MoodyPublishers.com

ISBN-13: 978-0-8024-3201-8

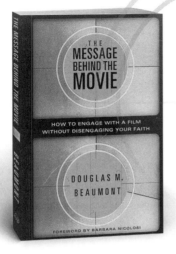

THE
MESSAGE
BEHIND THE
MOVIE

Christian books on movies often expose Hollywood's messages without teaching what to do about them or how to turn those messages into opportunities for sharing the gospel. In contrast, with this book readers will be able to understand the basics of movie interpretation, identify and interpret key ideas, and provide an uncomplicated defense of the Christian worldview.

In a fun and approachable style, apologetics professor and lover of movies Douglas Beaumont enables all of us to wisely engage with a film—to engage our culture without disengaging from our faith.

DOUGLAS M. BEAUMONT

MOODY
PUBLISHERS

MoodyPublishers.com